Christmas Presence

Christmas Presence

Twelve Gifts That Were More Than They Seemed

Edited by Gregory F. Augustine Pierce

ACTA
ASSISTING CHRISTIANS TO ACT
PUBLICATIONS

Christmas Presence
Twelve Gifts That Were More Than They Seemed
Edited by Gregory F. Augustine Pierce

Cover design and photo by Tom A. Wright
Typesetting by Desktop Edit Shop, Inc.

Copyright © 2002 by ACTA Publications

Published by: ACTA Publications
                Assisting Christians To Act
                4848 N. Clark Street
                Chicago, IL 60640-4711
                773-271-1030
                ACTAPUBLICATIONS@aol.com

Library of Congress Catalog Number: 2002092795
ISBN: 0-87946-237-X
Printed in the United States of America
Year: 08 07 06 05 04 03 02
Printing: 10 9 8 7 6 5 4 3 2 1

Contents

Dedication

To Monsignor Jack Egan,
a great Chicago priest,
who believed in the Incarnation...
and acted as if he did
every day of his life.

Introduction

Ah, Christmas presents! Children wait impatiently for them with great anticipation, adults search for them with determination (often mixed with frustration), and everyone tears them open with enthusiasm as soon as the signal is finally given. And then for the most part they are quickly forgotten—put on shelves, packed into boxes, eventually making their way to a garage sale, second-hand store or trashbin.

All except a few, that is. In each of our lives, there has been at least one special present that transcended its immediate value and even the intent of the giver. It may have been great or small, modest or invaluable, expected or not. But it was a gift that was more than it seemed, a gift that had another gift lying just beneath its surface, a gift that we never forgot because it revealed to us the essence of Christmas—the divine presence that permeates the world.

I received such a gift one winter in Chicago.

My wife, Kathy, and I had trouble having children, and so we were delighted when our twins, Abby and Nate, were born in 1987 (on my fortieth birthday no less). We were as delighted when we got pregnant again right away with our third child, Zack.

With three children under twenty months, however, the reality of the hard work of parenting hit us: the feeding, the diapers, the baths, the crying, the rocking, the sleeping. I should say the trying to sleep—the trying to get them to sleep (especially at the same time) and the trying to get a few minutes of sleep ourselves.

Unfortunately for us, our three babies (who are now teenagers) were terrible sleepers, right from the beginning. Perhaps it had something to do with the fact that there were so many of them at once. They would wake one another up or vie for feeding time waiting for a turn at Kathy's breast or for a bottle to warm up. All I know is that during that particular period in my life I watched more David Letterman (when he was on from midnight to two A.M.) than I have seen before or since, always carrying at least one baby in my arms who was most unhappy. I now tell new fathers that they will be tired for the next five years and *then* they will get some rest.

One of the things that suffered during those years was my spiritual life. I was working at my job, helping Kathy whenever I was at home, and trying (mostly unsuccessfully) to stay somewhat involved in church and community activities. The few moments I had for myself were used mostly to "veg out" or to catch a few hours of sleep (until one of the kids woke up again with needs that only Kathy or I could meet). The idea of prayer or meditation or spiritual reading seemed a luxury at best and a joke most of the time. If I did try any spiritual exercise, I'm sure it didn't last long before I was long gone to slumber land.

I was just about at the end of my proverbial rope in December of 1989. The twins had just turned two, and Zack was about three months old. My sleep time and my spiritual life had both shrunk to what seemed virtual zero. I was exhausted, burnt out, feeling anything but the Christmas spirit.

That's when I received a direct answer to a prayer, and it changed my life.

On what seemed the tenth night in a row, I was up with a crying child in my arms. In this case it was my daughter, Abigail (which means, just for the record, "the joy of her father"). Kathy was probably feeding Zack, or maybe I was just trying to give her a chance to sleep, since she was even more tired than I was (assuming that was possible).

All I know is that I was trying to calm Abby down and keep her from awakening her two brothers, for then—as I knew from experience—all heck would break lose. So I took her downstairs and was walking her from room to room, rocking her in my arms, stroking her hair, trying every trick I had in my meager parenting repertoire. But for some reason that night (gas, nightmare, diaper pin sticking into her skin?), Abby was not to be consoled. She was crying, and she was crying loud enough to wake up you-know-who.

It was then that I reverted, almost instinctively, to prayer. It was that kind of direct communication with God that we humans use when we don't have time for niceties with the divine. It was me and God, *mano y mano*, no-holds-barred, no preliminaries, not even a healthy fear of the Lord on my part.

"I don't get it, God," I said, perhaps even aloud, since Abby was making enough noise to cover it up anyway. "I thought parenting was supposed to be a wonderful, uplifting, transcendent experience, but I don't see the spirituality in this at all. I am exhausted. I don't want to be up at three in the morning with another crying baby. I just want to go to sleep. This childrearing is nothing but work. I don't find it holy or sacred or meaningful at all. Please show me how you are present in all this crying and lack of sleep!"

Just then, Abby stopped crying. Something had caught her two-year-old attention. She was looking out the living room window at the streetlight in front of our house. She pointed at it, smiled, and said a single word: "Snow!"

To this day I don't know how she even knew the word, much less how she connected it with the white flakes falling outside. Her age was such that she couldn't have remembered the snow from the previous year, much less what it was called, and this was the first snowfall of the season.

I suddenly realized that the reason I was awake was to witness and share my child's discovery of the mystery and delight of snow. I had also been given an immediate and direct answer to my prayer. God was present: in the snow, in my children, in my work as a dad. I had but to look for that presence and be open to it.

That experience actually changed how I think about spirituality and my daily work. I no longer see them as separate or competing things. I recognize that all my work—on my job, with my family, in my church and community—will have plenty of "crying time." That is the nature of the human condition. But now I realize that God is always present, even in the midst of the most frustrating, physically or psychologically wearing, seemingly unproductive times.

The gift of a crying child allowed me to recognize the sacred in my daily life.

This memory led me to wonder if other people had a story of a gift they had received that turned out to be more than it seemed at the time. I remembered the carol "The Twelve Days of Christmas" and decided to ask twelve of my favorite writers if they had such a story they could give to me, and each one did:

- **Kass Dotterweich** gave me a story about Christmas shopping in the mall of the heart. "When my son Joseph was five years old," she says, "he went on a shopping spree that none of us will ever forget. He certainly did not have the money to buy presents for both his parents and his five siblings. Nor did he have the crafty wherewithal to construct something homemade for each of us. Instead, Joseph did his Christmas shopping at home—and this was way before the advent of the Internet."
- **Tom McGrath** recalled the story of the year his dad

signed up to teach religious education to eighth graders. "As a sixth grader at the time," Tom notes, "I saw these guys as bullies, hooligans and ne'er-do-wells. They smoked, spit, used foul language on the playground and wore their hair like James Dean. I was convinced they were irredeemable. My dad thoroughly enjoyed the classes, however, and I couldn't understand why—until a week or so before Christmas, when I accompanied Dad and his class to deliver food to people in a poor neighborhood."

- **Father James (Jeff) Behrens** offered the story of ten lost Christmas stockings—stockings that symbolized "that we humans are filled with good things that have been 'emptied out' of God. Now it is our turn to empty ourselves to fill the larger world with good things."

- **Alice Camille** described a present from one of her nieces who had just developed her sense of irony. "Gifts that children cobble together and give—out of scraps of paper, ingenuity and love—are the best of all," Alice proclaims. "From my nieces over the years, I've gotten a various assortment of poems, bookmarks and curious items hard to define. But the year of the toaster goes down as the most amazing testament to love ever to come my way at Christmas time."

- **Michael Leach** reprised a story his sons want to hear over and over. "Our two boys are men now," he explains. "It's Christmas Day, and they want to hear again about their first Christmas in Connecticut, that historic day in 1972 when the snow was higher than a reindeer's antlers and their parents opened a fortune cookie beneath the

Christmas tree."

- **Father Pat Hannon** produced the story of the floppy-eared puppy, Buddy, whom he schemed to get for Christmas one year. "This convoluted strategy," he reports, "culminated on my eighth Christmas in a gift clumsily wrapped in the Sunday funnies, a gift—as I was to discover years only years later—that changed the entire direction of my life."

- **Delle Chatman** told of the worst year of her life and how a visit to her grandmother's homestead healed her soul. "When Grandmother suddenly plunked back into my life," Delle recalls, "the Hollywood lifestyle that had consumed every ounce of my devotion found a familial foundation that grounded me in reality again."

- **Fred Hang** described his unique nativity scene. "Every Christmas for the past several years," he begins, "I have placed a tiny ceramic frog in the manger. But to understand why, you have to know how the whole frog thing got started.

- **Carol DeChant** mined the significance of a camera that her Aunt Harriet had given her when Carol was eight. "My aunt had married too late in life to have children," she says. "So, unfamiliar with kids as she was, she didn't know any better than to give me something that was not (as we say today) age-appropriate. Thank goodness, because that Brownie Hawkeye transformed me from a gawky, self-conscious kid into my comic-book hero, Invisible Scarlet O'Neil."

- **John Shea** contributed the fictional story of a Christmas kaleidoscope that was literally more than meets the eye. "It was a large kaleidoscope," he relates. "The casing was real wood, a dark stained oak that gave it a polished, handsome look. It came with a stand that made a clear statement: 'I am not an ordinary, budget-bin kaleidoscope. I belong in a prominent place, displayed on a table or shelf. I do not deserve the back of the closet and, under no circumstances, should I disappear beneath the bed.'"

- **Patrick Reardon** told of one Christmas gift that he keeps before him all the time. "It's a representative of a type of gift that never disappoints," he explains. "It always leaves me feeling loved, filled with joy and life, as happy as a lord-a-leaping. I keep it on my dresser because it stands for all those other cards and notes and communications that, in our family, we give each other day in and day out. It represents all the gestures of affection that are part of our everyday lives together—the hugs, the kisses and the frequent bald statements of love that we exchange."

- **Vinita Wright** had a collection of remembrances—of weather and religion, of tradition, family and food. "The word *Christmas*," she announces, "causes me to remember, first of all, that ancient narrative of my faith: that God came to earth as a little baby, wrapped up and placed on a straw bed, his young mother miles from her homeland, his father disturbed by dreams." But when Vinita goes a little deeper into that story, she discovers other stories as well. "They have grown out of that original story, but their characters and settings and plots are from my own life."

These are all, indeed, stories that remind us of the very reason we give gifts at Christmas. We do so to put us in touch with the mystery of the divine spirit who was incarnated, took on flesh, became a human being. Because of the birth of Jesus, we now know we can touch that divine spirit through the material world—of cameras, frogs, toasters, kaleidoscopes...and snow and crying babies.

The Incarnation—the presence of God in our world—is the essence of Christmas.

Christmas Shopping in the Mall of the Heart

Kass Dotterweich

ow we all long to live the true spirit of Advent—the spirit of awareness, anticipation and acceptance that prepares the human heart for the Feast of the Incarnation. We want to fashion our own inner crèche for the gentle coming of the Light of the World and let our love for each other become, as mystic and poet Caryll Houselander puts it, "the four walls that shelter him."

The pressures of our culture, however, often leave our longing awash in a sea of counter-Advent realities. Let's face it: Christmas takes preparation...and perspiration. In the weeks before December 25, we find ourselves flustered and frazzled with the rush of details that, if left unattended, will in some way make our celebration of the holiday less than what we project it to be.

Not so with my son Joseph, at least not that Advent season over twenty years ago, when he was seven years old.

Now, of my six children Joseph is definitely the one who hears most clearly that "different drummer." He finds his way through life by putting one foot in front of the other in a rhythm that simply does not seem to conform to the expected.

Early one Sunday afternoon that December, Joseph had the privilege of lighting the third candle on our Advent wreath, displaying his evident pride in being the one to light the "pretty pink one" that symbolizes our rejoicing in the ever-nearer arrival of the baby Jesus. Perhaps I should have seen something on the horizon right then, so serious was Joseph in his privileged status as the lighter of the candle of hope.

My years of being Mom had taught me that if my children are not hurting themselves or others and are not about to destroy some treasured object, then I don't ask questions. After all, the childhood imagination needs its freedom if it is to learn to fly.

Later that evening, I noticed him moving through the dining room with a most inquisitive look on his face. He strolled, he bent and stooped, he got down on his belly to take a look under the china cabinet. He then began to rummage, digging into the clutter on the top of the dining room table and pulling out the drawers in the buffet—clearly in search of something. Within a short period of time, however, Joseph left the room with a mild display of frustration.

My years of being Mom had taught me that if my children are not hurting themselves or others and are not about to destroy some treasured object, then I don't ask questions. After all, the childhood imagination needs its freedom if it is to learn to fly. Whatever Joseph was doing was clearly harmless. And if he needed my assistance, he'd surely ask.

For days after, I observed this peculiar behavior from Joseph many times over...and in every room in the house. He would stroll through a room, rummage through cluttered countertops and drawers, wiggle under beds, dig through closet floors, reach under chairs—always disturbing dust and debris that had been neglected or forgotten or ignored for a very long time.

When my curiosity finally peaked a few days before Christmas, I gave in to what I knew would be a brief and fruitless exchange. "Joseph, what are you doing when you roam through the house digging through stuff?"

"Huh? Oh, um, nothing," he responded sheepishly, seemingly embarrassed that his odd routine had even been noticed.

Finally, Christmas Eve day dawned. As is the custom in our family, the Christmas tree went up and underneath went the presents—things from grandparents and aunts and uncles that had been arriving in the mail over the weeks. At one point, I noticed Joseph bringing out his presents for all of us and putting them under the tree as well. Suddenly, my heart experienced a surge of a mother's greatest fear—the fear of the unknown.

What was Joseph putting under the tree? And not so much what, but how? Joseph didn't have any spending money, and he definitely was not inclined toward make-every-body-something craft activity. Add to that the fact that Joseph had been known to engage in a little shoplifting from time to time, and I experienced a major maternal panic.

After the family went to Mass and shared a small breakfast, it was time to gather around the tree to see what surprises nestled there waiting to delight one and all.

I spent a rather tense Christmas Eve that year, worrying about what "presents" Joseph was giving his parents and siblings. I was haunted by the memory of a conversation with the manager of a local department store six weeks earlier. She had accused my child of slipping an eraser into his coat pocket—an accusation that eventually proved true. Joseph had, indeed, taken the eraser. Why? "Because Jimmy has one just like it," he explained in all innocence, failing completely to see the moral nuances that were so obvious to me.

I also remembered an afternoon in late autumn of that year when Joseph somehow had enough candy bars to "share" with all his siblings. Investigation had led me to the corner convenience store where I learned that Joseph had, indeed, been seen acting furtively there (much like he had been around the house recently).

That Christmas Eve, my last conscious thought before drifting off to troubled sleep was that maybe I should open a couple of Joseph's presents and see for myself what was going on. Instead, I merely repeated my Advent mantra over and over again: "Come, Lord Jesus, and do not delay. Give courage to your people today."

Christmas morning dawned and, despite my apprehension, the festivities began. After the family went to Mass and shared a small breakfast, it was time to gather around the tree to see what surprises nestled there waiting to delight one and all. One by one, the presents were handed out, and one by one, recipients pulled at bows, ripped at paper, and glowed with satisfaction as some new treasure came to the surface.

Through it all, Joseph was a bundle of anticipation...and so was his mother. As the mountain of packages under the tree dwindled, Joseph's presents for others became more and more obvious—his wrappings of old newspaper and miles of adhesive tape set his gifts apart.

Instinctively, we all avoided the unavoidable, until Joseph finally exploded, "Can I give everybody my presents now?"

I swallowed hard, sat perfectly still, and focused on how best to handle the situation when the truth became evident.

"Sure, Joe. Go ahead," I said, thinking to myself, "Might as well get this over with."

"Here, Christine. This is for you," Joseph offered with flushed anticipation, handing his oldest sister a small, bulky bundle and moving in close for a good view of her reaction. Clearly, Joseph knew his sister was going to be delighted— and that disturbed me greatly.

Christine, thirteen at the time, looked at Joseph with perhaps not the same kind of misgivings I was experiencing but perplexity nonetheless. "Thanks, Joey," she said as she peeled away layers of tape and crinkly newspaper.

Oh, how I held my breath for the hit. I was already rehearsing how to get the information I would need from Joseph. "Oh, honey, how nice. Where did you get that? Did Grandma go shopping with you? Help you pick it out? Pay for it?"

Within seconds, however, Christine's eyes were dancing with glee as she held up a hairbrush—her hairbrush, the one that had been missing for weeks, the one that she'd painfully grieved because it was the only one that "worked."

Joseph, ignoring Christine's queries of "Where did you find it?" then made a dive for the next present and handed his oldest brother, Jerome, what looked like a shoebox. Again, within seconds, Jerome was grinning from ear to ear as he held up his Little League cleats, missing since right before the playoff games late the previous August. "Cool man! Where were they?"

And so it went. Present after present was handed out with high anticipation, and present after present brought surprise and wonder. Each family member rediscovered a treasured object that had somehow been lost, misplaced or forgotten in a chaotic household of eight people.

🖌️

As for my present? Joseph had taken from the corner of my home workdesk a small porcelain Madonna and Child statue I had picked up at a yard sale years earlier for fifty cents. I never noticed the statue anymore. According to Joseph he'd taken it from my desk weeks earlier, and I never even missed it. Quite frankly, it was just a little piece of junk to me.

Today, however, that little statue is a sacred object enshrined in my curio, where I display my especially treasured heirlooms. My son had shopped in the mall of the heart and had brought home to me two precious gifts that I didn't even know I wanted...or needed.

First, in his innocence Joseph had reminded me that the Incarnation is not so much about God's giving of some *thing* to the world but rather it is about divine life permeating *all things*. Christmas is not about some newness entering into the world—something that wasn't there one minute and is the next—but rather it is the celebration of the Spirit that gives to all of us what in fact we already have. Christmas gift giving merely celebrates our essential humanity. Those gifts that are ours in the moment of creation and in the moment of our own conception are the essence of peace.

Joseph also gave me a renewed appreciation for the joy of surprise. With great sadness I admit here, decades later, that I had been watching my son through a mother's critical eyes—not through a mother's eyes of wonder. I had shut down on my own child's potential for good and focused only on his limitations, expecting something disturbing instead of delightful. Through the long hours of that entire Christmas Eve day, I hadn't even "hoped" for something good. Rather, by making assumptions about what I considered the inevitable I had robbed myself of the graces of anticipation and expectation.

Joseph also gave me a renewed appreciation for the joy of surprise.

I continue to marvel at the priceless present Joseph gave me that Christmas morning. It was certainly more than a recycled fifty-cent statue. It was a reminder of the essence of peace and the appreciation of surprise that we all possess but somehow fail to notice.

Dad's Gift

Tom McGrath

My dad has always been a natural teacher, and so it wasn't surprising that someone at the parish would put "the arm" on him to teach religious education. One September, many years ago, a nun called and asked if he'd take over a class of eighth-grade boys.

Dad threw himself into the challenge with enthusiasm. He would prepare his lessons with ingenuity and care, constantly dreaming up ways to entice the dry bones of eternal truths to come to life in the hearts and imaginations of his charges. He spent evenings dressing up the skeletal outlines laid out in the teacher's manual. He drew arrows and notes and comments ("Tell them this!"), making a cheat sheet of stories and arguments that might illuminate the way to faith. He tried to pour out what was bubbling up in his heart into fifty-minute lesson plans.

I was proud of my father and his flair for teaching. Yet I couldn't understand why he had agreed to teach eighth-grade CCD. I was in sixth grade at the Catholic school, but I knew all about those public-school eighth graders: They smoked, they spit, they swore, they talked dirty to the girls and made them blush, they wore their hair slicked back like James Dean.

I took it upon myself to let Dad know what kind of boys he would be dealing with, but he wouldn't listen. "Oh, Jimmy O'Brien? I knew him when he was in diapers. He's a good kid…." Then he would trail off, the "but" unspoken. Each week Dad continued to spend time poring over the teacher's manual and the Bible and even digging out his old books from his seminary days. He was clearly enjoying teaching these boys religion, much to my eleven-year-old surprise.

The weeks went along, I looked for signs of disaffection on Dad's part, but I saw none. If anything, he grew more enthused about his class by the week. As nostalgia for summer turned into longing for the Christmas holidays, a canned-goods drive was launched in the religious education program. Someone (my Dad? the nun in charge?) decided that gathering food and bringing it to the poor would be a good way to teach the students how to put their faith into action.

How could public-school kids be as generous as those of us who went to Catholic school every day?

My young mind figured the effort would flop, given the nature of the kids, but each week Dad reported how the jumbo collection boxes were filling up with stockpiles of canned goods and toys. Still, something seemed fishy to me. How could public-school kids be as generous as those of us who went to Catholic school every day?

We were scheduled to deliver the food on the Saturday before Christmas. (I say "we" because Dad made it clear that I was to help, even though I wasn't even in his class.) That day was also the first winter snowfall in Chicago. Big thick flakes floated oh-so-lazily from a low gray sky, covering our neighborhood with an inviting blanket of white.

It would soon become a good day for two of my favorite pastimes: making snow forts and storing up dozens of hard-packed snowballs—just in case. My friends, I knew, would be trudging up and down the block, sleds in tow, looking for me, but I had to go out with a bunch of juvenile delinquents and deliver Christmas baskets!

I waited in the steamy heat of our kitchen for Dad to get home from work, watching the snow begin to fall in earnest.

He bustled in, shoulders full of snow, a smile on his face. His hand was cold on my forehead as he tousled my hair and asked if I was ready. Clearly I was not as ready as he was.

At the parish parking lot, most of the teachers and students from the religious education program had gathered and were loaded into cars. Seven of the eighth-grade guys jammed into the back of our car, squeezing me into a tight space over the hump in the back seat. Dad's '54 Ford was a tank with no ventilation, and I felt smothered by wet wool and the breath of guys who'd spent their morning standing around smoking. Snow slowed the traffic and we seemed to inch along for hours.

At a certain point, we pulled off the main shopping streets and onto less traveled side streets. Suddenly, silence and calm came over the car. Through arms and armpits I could barely see outside the car window to a world that had been blessed and beautified by snow. We pulled up at our first stop—not a parish, which I guess is what I had expected, but an apartment building.

We all got out of the car, opened the trunk, and stood around, embarrassed and uncertain what to do next. Dad quickly took over and led the charge. He gave us each something to carry and we made our way to the first address on his list. An old woman opened the door a crack. She was frightened and suspicious, even when Dad laid on the old Irish charm. He understood why she might be uncomfortable, and we left the food on the landing outside her doorway, wished her Merry Christmas, and thumped our way back down the stairs. As we got to the bottom landing, we heard her rummaging through the bags. And then she yelled from above, "God bless you! God bless you boys!"

At the next stop we met a tired young mother with a bunch of kids who were running wild through the apartment. It wasn't clear whether or not these were all hers. She showed no emotion when we arrived, seemingly resigned to whatever twists and turns life would send her next. We all stood at the door feeling awkward, but then Dad got her talking. Yes, she knew Father McGinty from the local parish. "Oh, he gave you my name? Well, would you like to come in and have a cup of coffee? I think I have some cookies around here someplace for the boys."

> *I noticed that Dad's students were uncommonly subdued. There was no flash, no swagger, no attitude.*

So we brought the bags and boxes in. I noticed that Dad's students were uncommonly subdued. There was no flash, no swagger, no attitude. One of the kids from the house, a little boy about five, stood face to face with Stuart, the leader of Dad's pack of hoodlums. The little boy stood stone still for some time and then—moved by some primordial urge— flung his metal toy truck right at Stuart's head. I gasped, figuring the kid was in for it now. A sneer did cross Stuart's face, but then the look passed. He knelt down and got eye level with the kid. He smiled and said, "Some kinda arm you got there. You like baseball?"

And then Stuart reached into the shopping bag he had been carrying and took out a rubber ball. "Here," he said. "This is for you."

The boy grabbed the ball, hugged it with both hands to his chest, and did a little dance of joy. We all laughed—Dad, his gang of ne'er-do-wells, and me—and the mother and the other children in the family laughed too. We boys spent a little time showing the kids their new toys and playing with them while Dad had a cup of coffee with the lady. They were visiting as if they were long lost family members.

We finally left the family and then stopped at three other homes that day, each time meeting people we never expected to meet—recent immigrants, people in "broken homes," people I'd looked down on from the "el" as we rode by on our way to see a movie or go shopping. We went into neighborhoods I had always passed through in fear, breathing easier only when I got back to my familiar turf again.

Someone expressed amazement at the weather and we all turned our faces to the sky. The snow circled above us under the street lamps like the inside of a shake-up globe.

When we pulled up at our last stop, snow was continuing to fall unabated. The other boys and I milled around the back of the car. They were beginning to include me in their number. An elevated train roared by at the end of the block, shaking all the apartments lined up next to it. A couple of kids were dragging a skinny Christmas tree up the front stoop of their three-flat. Down the block a menacing looking group of men were standing around some double-parked cars. One of the men got the attention of his companion and nodded toward our crowd. I got scared, then I heard a shout.

Dad looked up, and the smile broadened into a boyish grin. "Holy smokes!" he cried. "If it isn't 'The Professor' himself." (Dad has nicknames for everybody.) He left us standing there and walked toward the men. Soon there were handshakes and shoulder slaps and smiles all around. One of the men worked with Dad, and Dad soon called us over and introduced us. The men shook our hands and we all attempted a few jokes, which were followed by polite chuckles. Someone expressed amazement at the weather and we all turned our faces to the sky. The snow circled above us under the street lamps like the inside of a shake-up globe.

One of the cars the men had been working on had a bad ignition switch. They were about to maneuver it out into the street and push it to a running start, so all of us boys joined in this exciting (but foolhardy) effort. Slipping and sliding along the street, we got the car moving at a decent clip and the guy behind the wheel popped the clutch and the motor turned over. The man waved wildly out the driver-side window, fishtailing his way down the street, and one of the guys called out something in Spanish and the men all laughed. My Dad asked what they'd said and his co-worker explained, "He told the guy, 'Don't stop until you get to Guadalajara!'"

After that, the men brought out beer and soda and we all stood around having a drink. It no longer seemed cold. Kids from the neighborhood came by and we chatted.

When it was time to get going, Dad asked his friend if he

knew the family we were supposed to deliver to next. He did. They were related to his wife. Dad said, "Could you do us a favor? I've got something that belongs to them. Could you make sure they get it? Just some stuff for Christmas."

"I will," the man said. "We're bringing them a ham later today anyway."

When we piled back into the car, the guys laid me across their lap and teased me about being so small. I laughed along with them. I even cracked a few jokes and got them laughing. I began to see them as their family members probably saw them—as goofy but good boys. When we got back to the parish parking lot it felt good to be out in the open air again. The guys stood around, no one wanting to leave. We stood for a few minutes looking at each other as snow piled up on heads and shoulders. All around us, it fell in abundance, and there seemed to be no other place any of us would rather be.

> Now, my heart was bigger and I was ready for Christmas.

Finally, the boys all shook my Dad's hand and wished him a merry Christmas. Then they shook mine, too. Dad reminded them he'd like to see them at Mass Christmas morning. "We'll see about that, Mr. McGrath," they said and laughed, but somehow I got the feeling that we might just see them there.

"Thanks for taking us today," said Stuart, speaking for the gang. "It wasn't stupid like we thought it would be."

"No," said Dad. "It wasn't stupid at all."

When Dad and I got home, the Christmas tree lights were on and the house smelled of dinner on the stove. Mom had me slip into warm jeans and a flannel shirt fresh from the dryer. Dickens' *A Christmas Carol*—the good one with Alistair Sims—was on TV. I sat on the couch feeling surprisingly full, since I hadn't eaten since breakfast. I had been out in the world, and now I was home. Only now, my heart was bigger and I was ready for Christmas.

Years before that Christmas, when my Dad would come home from work in the summer, all the little kids in the neighborhood—Steve and Jan and Jeffery and Susie and everybody—would run madly down the street and into his arms. He would swoop them up and hold them high above his head and call them by name.

The day we delivered Christmas presents to the poor, I finally realized that what Dad was doing each week with his religious education class was swooping the boys up and holding them high and calling them by name—just as he always did with me.

That has always been his gift.

The Christmas Stockings

James Stephen Behrens

My memories of Christmas are many and flow from the beauty of gift giving and gift receiving. Above all, of course, is the ultimate gift to humanity—a child born in poverty and dying in disgrace whom we came to recognize as God himself. Yes, the gift of Christmas is the gift of our very salvation.

Not long ago I was sitting in the church at a monastery and thinking about how easy it is to approach salvation as a one-time event that happened a long time ago. The thought struck me that we are all somehow part of salvation history, that something wonderful is happening right now in and through us because of the birth of Jesus.

As I looked about me that morning at the monks and heard the sweet songs of the birds in the cloister and the occasional whine of a jet passing overhead, I realized that salvation is continuing to happen right now—as I write this and eventually as you read it. Christmas wasn't a one-time event that we remember every December 25, it is unfolding continuously through the small slice of eternity that we humans experience as time, and our annual Advent and Christmas observance is merely our celebration of the salvation that is occurring throughout the year.

How is it that we share in salvation? I think it is so simple, so everyday, that we usually do not even notice it.

How is it that we share in salvation? I think it is so simple, so everyday, that we usually do not even notice it. But it is there, behind the ordinary course of any given day. It is there, working its way through our hands and hearts, the birds and machines and the joys and sorrows of life. I see this truth most clearly in the small gifts of Christmas, like ones I received each year in my Christmas stocking.

There were ten of us at home when I was growing up in a big house on Christopher Street in Montclair, New Jersey: Grandma, Mom and Dad, me and my twin brother, Jimmy, Johnny, Mary, Robert, Meg and Peter. On Christmas Eve, Mom always hung stockings above the fireplace in the living room. They were special stockings that she had bought during a Christmas season many years ago. They were made of red felt and had a white band across the top and a sprig of green felt holly. Each stocking had a tab and through the tab Mom stuck a thumbtack and attached the stockings to the white mantelpiece. The stockings were placed in the exact order of our earthly arrival, and the holes left by the thumb tacks reminded me throughout the year of the good feelings of the holidays.

On Christmas morning, the stockings would be filled with candies and small little gifts that Mom and Dad had picked out carefully and specifically for each of us. They were filled from top to bottom, so that the toe part of the stockings bulged from the weight of the goodness that had been placed therein. I remember there were always pencils and pens and drawing things for me. My sisters and brothers received things given especially for their passions or hobbies. We all received sweet candy canes and candies shaped like ribbons. The gifts in the stockings were small in size, but their size had nothing to do with how important they were to us.

Those stockings were a sign of continuity in our family. Each year, they were filled with more "mature" things as Christmases came and went. But the stockings remained the same. The reds and greens never faded, and when a hole in the mantle became too large and overused and no longer able to hold a tack, there was always plenty of room for a new one.

We sold the house in Montclair in 1974, after Jimmy had died in a car crash during high school. We moved to

Connecticut and the stockings came along with us and easily found a new place above the new fireplace in the new house. And so it was that for another decade or so the stockings were hung and filled each Christmas. We always hung Jimmy's, right next to mine.

Mom and Dad decided to retire to Louisiana in 1980, and all the belongings from their entire married life together had to be packed and shipped. Much of the "stuff," however, had to be tossed. The Christmas stockings were in a special box in the garage, where they awaited being picked up by my brother Peter, who was going to drive the car to Louisiana. One morning, however, Mom walked into the garage and the box was gone.

Every place that a Behrens inhabits at Christmas has stockings hung somewhere.

She realized that the garbage men had probably come in and mistaken the box for trash and taken it away. Mom was beside herself. It was as if the only ten sure places she could fill with love each year were forever gone. We never saw them again.

The years have passed. Jimmy, Gram and Dad are now gone. My sisters and brothers are scattered all over the country and Mom lives in an assisted-living home in Louisiana. Every place that a Behrens inhabits at Christmas, however, has stockings hung somewhere. They are all new, of course, but it is as if the ten originals have given way to offspring of their own.

And every year, Mom is given stockings filled to the brim by each of us. And we all know that she gives away those filled stockings to her friends (and probably to some strangers, too). So the overflowing of love that began so many years ago on Christopher Street continues and multiplies.

Mom and Dad probably never dreamed that I would take their Christmas-stocking gifts to heart the way I have. The little things they crammed into those stockings are still with me. They still have life—as if they had finally taught me their lessons over the years. Why do I love to write so much? Partly, I am convinced, because my parents loved me enough to include pencils and paper in my Christmas stockings.

Good things take time to take root in our lives. They must be repeated, over and over again, until they become part of our very being. I did not think much, if at all, about these patterns when I was younger. I did not realize that the filling of our days and years and lifetimes with love are what brings about salvation.

I like to think that it is ultimately God who does the filling. As sure as he filled the universe with matter and this relatively small planet (at least) with life, he also filled the hearts of my parents as they shopped for small, meaningful things with which to fill our Christmas stockings. By the time our stockings were lost for good, what they had given over the years had already been received.

Perhaps of all the gospel writers, John best develops the theme of God's emptying the divine life into the life of the flesh ("The Word became flesh, and dwelt amongst us"). Indeed, the fourth gospel lays out the entire plan of salvation: that all things shall eventually be filled with grace and brought back to God.

Things eternal seeped through the crevices and cracks of that home on Christopher Street and filled the human lives therein.

These are lofty thoughts, indeed. Earth is such an insignificant place in the vast expanse of the universe, but the angels came and all creation bowed low here on that first Christmas night, when heaven was wedded forever to our little world. Little did I know when growing up that the same mystery was taking place in our lives when our parents tacked up those Christmas stockings each Christmas Eve. Things eternal seeped through the crevices and cracks of that home on Christopher Street and filled the human lives therein.

I am grateful for the grace that came to everyone in my family through those stockings. That was my parents' real gift to us. They emptied themselves that we might know the joy of receiving, and by so doing they taught us as well the joy of giving through emptying ourselves for others. And now I realize that this same emptying is God's gift to us all, and that is what we celebrate each year at Christmas.

I have with me a photograph taken on Christmas Eve of 1962. We are all there, huddled together on a couch, including Jimmy and Grandma, with Dad crouching before the couch on his knees, smiling at the camera. I do not remember who took the picture, for all ten of us are in it. To the left is the piano and to the right stands the Christmas tree. Had the lens been just a little bit larger, the photo would have included the Christmas stockings. They are not in the picture, however. Like what eventually happened to them, they are out of sight forever.

But it doesn't matter. It would be nice to have them still, or at least a picture of them. But I see in the image of my family what those stockings meant and still mean. We humans are filled with good things that have been "emptied out" of God. Now it is our turn to empty ourselves to fill the larger world with good things.

The Year of the Toaster

Alice Camille

illy Aunt Alice!" I don't know who first gave me this title or remember under what circumstances my silliness was initially revealed. But *silly* has been more than an adjective used to describe me for ten years and counting. It's part of my name. Just ask my nieces.

My sister Ida sighs when her children call out to me in this irreverent way. "If only they knew you like I do," she says, shaking her head. "You are the unsilliest, the most truly serious person I know."

Perhaps I come across as serious because I've worked in ministry of one stripe or another for twenty years now. In and out of parishes, Newman Centers, homeless shelters and religious education classes—a lot of my career has been about serious stuff like helping people find God and getting desperate folk out of the rain. I admit, there's nothing lighthearted about grieving with people who've lost a loved one or trying to build a bridge of hope for a teenager pregnant for the third time. But it would not be accurate to say, simply because I take part in the very sobering business of life,

---

that I am a serious person.

The life of faith I take with utmost gravity. Myself, however, I try to ride like a soap bubble. Francis of Assisi's Holy Fool seems to me to make sense as a model for my discipleship. So far, I've got the fool part down just right.

Hanging with kids is the best antidote to the lure of self-importance that I can think of. Kids are great for developing your humility and unleashing the power of play. That's why Christmas at my sister's house in Pennsylvania is every bit as good for me as being a kid again myself. My three nieces dominate the scene with their exuberant sense of fun. It is one of the few places where I feel free enough to get the giggles and express them—without raising eyebrows or losing esteem, for what that's worth.

> *Kids are great for developing your humility and unleashing the power of play.*

I suppose the Silly Aunt business started early, when Megan was five, Amanda three, and Mary still in the crib. I would say during a conversation with my sister and within earshot of the kids (and without the slightest change of tone) the most foolish thing I could think of. For example: "Of course, we will be having *dragons* with our dinner?"

Little Amanda would pause, staggered by the idea.

"Dragons for dinner?" she'd ask without guile.

Meanwhile Megan, only slightly older but hip to the whole concept of irony well before she entered kindergarten, would rejoin calmly, "With *lemon sauce,* I hope!"

By the time Mary was old enough to join in our word-play, the pattern was established: Under no circumstances was anything Aunt Alice said to be taken seriously!

And so it came to pass one Christmas as Megan picked up a present under the tree with her name on it, I yawned and said, "That should be the toaster. It looks about the right size."

"Of course!" Megan replied with feigned delight. "Just what I wanted—a toaster!"

"Naturally," I agreed. "What young girl doesn't dream of receiving her first toaster?"

Amanda tilted her head doubtfully. "But little girls don't want toasters," she began. And then she hesitated, unwilling to pursue her line of argument further under such evident social pressure. Amanda was caught in that hapless developmental stage educators call "concrete-operational." That is, she maintained a steadfast literal perspective whenever metaphor limped past her dragging its leg—a hunchback orphaned from the world of meaning. Irony, gags and winks found no home in Amanda. She listened hard, but she could not hear past the solidity of words that suddenly had become unreliable in a way she couldn't penetrate.

"At least *I* don't want a toaster," she concluded, finding some peace in registering that certainty. And she seemed even more relieved when the present in question turned out to be a Happy Rainbow nightlight rather than a kitchen-counter appliance.

Unfortunately for Amanda, however, the toaster gag didn't go away. Each Christmas from that year forward, someone picked up on the joke when the right-shaped gift came along: "Could this *finally* be the toaster?"

And Megan would swoon in pre-teen melodramatic tones: "If *only* someone, someday, would give me my own toaster!" Amanda remained stumped by this game, her face in a knot, expressing incredulity that children should ever be given toast-

Like everyone else, I'd pretend to be disappointed when the small appliance did not appear from underneath the wrappings.

ers, much less that any kid would really want one. Annoyed and frustrated when people laughed at the ongoing joke, Amanda got even more upset when little Mary got in on the act. Mary would start giggling each time I'd select a gift with my name on it: "Silly Aunt Alice, are you gonna get a toaster this year?"

"I certainly *hope* so." I'd say. And like everyone else, I'd pretend to be disappointed when the small appliance did not appear from underneath the wrappings.

Perhaps five Christmases went by before Amanda finally cultivated her appreciation for irony and joined in the game with us. But because she had suffered at the expense of the joke for so long, the tradition took on iconic status for her. It had been her opponent every holiday, and now she needed a way to prove herself the master of it.

So on the Christmas after she turned ten, it was time for Amanda to turn the tables. I've got to hand it to her: She was one cool character that Christmas morning—sitting and playing board games with her sisters on the floor quite innocently as the grownups cooked and set the tables. People kept arriving and pouring bags of packages under the tree, while the wonderful smells of ham and bread and desserts filled the air. I chatted with the kids here and there, teasing as always, and Amanda teased back with the best of them.

"Maybe I'll finally get my toaster this year," I said casually, winking at Amanda.

"Maybe you will," she replied just as casually.

I suspected nothing. That coy little actress! Her heart must have been thumping madly in her chest all morning, exhilarated with the thought of her triumph to come. But she never gave it away.

After the meal, we assembled under the tree for the familiar ritual of passing the gifts around. Our holiday family is large, and opening gifts can and usually does take hours. Each gift is opened with great ceremony, and the giver receives the proper appreciation. The living room becomes a wreck of colored paper, and leftover bows stick to people's socks for hours afterwards. Even the smallest kids usually have a drawing or school craft to offer, and some of the best moments come in deciphering what these handmade treasures are supposed to be.

> *The time arrived when I picked it up—the gift that must have been ticking like a time bomb in Amanda's imagination for weeks.*

The time arrived when I picked *it* up—the gift that must have been ticking like a time bomb in Amanda's imagination for weeks. It was rectangular, roughly the size and shape of a you-know-what, and it had my name on it. It was signed, in the most natural way possible: "Love, Amanda."

"I suppose this is my toaster," I called to her across the room to her. Everyone chuckled.

"You never know," she said gaily.

I undid the wrappings and my jaw dropped. My sister had the good sense to snap a picture. It captures my amazement, my laughter, my humility that the joke, at last, was on me. I laughed until the tears squeezed out at the corners of my eyes, and in the picture I'm hugging my niece until she's out of breath. Like the Cheshire Cat, she has become nothing but a white grin of pure pleasure. Her euphoria and my delight are all one thing, and between us in the photo is her ingenious creation.

Of course it was a toaster. But to say it was a toaster is like calling the Garden of Eden a nice lawn.

How a ten-year-old came up with a fully functional appliance from a cardboard box and two Popsicle sticks will remain a mystery to me. But Amanda's toaster is a thing of wonder. The corrugated box makes a nice sturdy frame for the two wide slits in the top. The exterior is painted radiator silver and shines in the light. Two squares of corrugated board are daubed white for the toast, and they rest perfectly, half in and half out of the slots, like breakfast ready to be served. On one end is the black Popsicle stick lever, attached perpendicularly to a second stick in the recesses of the machine. And honest to God, when you push down on the lever, the toast leaps into the air. Voila!

Everyone took turns flipping the toast out of the toaster all day that Christmas. Amanda sat meekly playing games with the other children, a strangely mature smile on her face. She knew she had done it; she had out-sillied her Aunt Alice. And she had done it with a cleverness that was beyond me.

Today the toaster sits on my desk at work. Whenever I am tempted to take things too seriously, I merely push down on the Popsicle lever and watch the white cardboard toast flip up and sail through the air.

Perhaps I had it backward all those years. What every *grownup* needs is her own toaster.

Christmas in Connecticut, 1972

Michael Leach

ell us about the time we had Chinese takeout for Christmas," says Chris. "Remember? The year Jeff was born."

"That was some thirty years ago, the year after you were born. You want to hear it again?" I ask.

"Yeah, Dad. Tell it again," Jeff pipes in. "Tell us about the best Christmas gift you and Mom ever had."

"You guys sound like Lennie in *Of Mice and Men:* 'Tell us about the rabbits, George. Tell us how it's gonna be.'"

"Tell us how it *was*," Chris says. "On Christmas Day, 1972."

Our two boys are men now. Their mother is in the kitchen cutting the pumpkin pie, and they want to hear about their first Christmas in Connecticut—that historic day when the snow was higher than a reindeer's antlers and their parents opened a fortune cookie beneath the Christmas tree.

"Alright then." I take off my glasses to better see the past. "Once upon a Christmas past when we had less money than the widow with her mite, we received a gift more precious than all the pearls in the ocean, all the stars in the sky."

"Easy, Mr. Sweetheart," says Mrs. Sweetheart as she brings in the steaming pie. "Why don't you tell it like it was?"

"No, Dad," says Jeff. "Tell it like you always tell it."

I continue. "We were poor then and lived in a little red barn house with a white picket fence on Havemeyer Lane. It was big enough for love though, and we had plenty of that."

"It was yellow, Dad. A yellow ranch house. Remember the vinyl siding?"

"Let your father talk, Chris. Go on, Sweets."

"A little yellow ranch house, but to us it was the Taj Mahal."

"Yes," their mom agrees. "That's the way it was."

"No, Mom," Chris says. "I drove by our old house the other day, and the vinyl is cracked and the white picket fence is down and they painted the shutters a god-awful green."

"When you were little I buried you under mountains of gold. The only way I knew you were there was from your laughter."

"The fence was a split rail," Jeff says. "Remember the roses that climbed all over it in the summer?"

"I remember it well, " I recall. "They had no thorns. And remember how in autumn an avalanche of leaves fell from the sky and you and Chris frolicked and I raked them into wonderful piles of red and gold and tossed them all over you like confetti?"

"I remember we had to help you rake," says Chris.

"That was later," I remind him, "when you were ten and twelve and strong like bulls. When you were little I buried you under mountains of gold. The only way I knew you were there was from your laughter. Anyway, where was I?"

"The best Christmas gift you and Mom ever had."

"Yes! Christmas Day, 1972. We had moved to Connecticut on July 1st, Chris's first birthday. On December 15th Jeff came from God like another sunbeam from heaven. I was in the delivery room helping your mother breathe when you suddenly appeared. It was a miracle. Tears ran down my eyes."

"Mine too," their mother adds. "It hurt like hell, and your father almost fainted."

The boys laugh. They always laugh at this part. "Go on, Dad, tell it the way you tell it!"

"Jeff, you were ten days old on Christmas day but still smelled as fresh and new as those roses on our white picket fence."

"He smelled of poop, Dad, admit it." Both boys are hunched over now.

"Still does," Chris adds. Their mother is laughing too.

As the laughter subsides, I continue, softly. "Snow fell like it never fell before or since on the night before Christmas, 1972. When we woke up and looked out the window we had to peer over powder halfway up the house. The huge oak trees leaned toward us like hulking ships with crystal cargoes dragging them down to the sea of white below."

"Easy, Dad, easy."

"You boys were too young then to know the false meaning of Christmas. Chris didn't run to the tree to open presents. A fresh snowfall was present enough. The first thing I did was take Jeff out of his crib and place him beneath the Christmas tree, right next to the stable. He wore a fuzzy little red outfit that zipped up the front and covered his body, a little Santa giving us the gift of himself. Mom held you in her arms, Chris, and we knelt beneath the tree and thanked God for all the good he had given us, for our little house on Havemeyer Lane that was big enough for love, and for the gift of being together as one."

> "You boys were too young then to know the false meaning of Christmas. A fresh snowfall was present enough."

"I remember all of us sitting on the couch that day," their mother remembers, "in front of the fireplace. We put Jeff in your arms, Chris, and you held him like he was a porcelain doll. You were so gentle with him, even though you were hardly two."

"I know. I remember the picture Dad took."

"When you got older, you tried to kill me," Jeff says.

"You stole my Kiss tee-shirt," Chris reminds him. "You deserved it."

It's an old routine, delivered with the comfort of brothers who are joined at the heart like Siamese twins.

"Tell us about the present now," says Jeff, "about the best gift you and Mom ever had."

"We did have a few presents under the tree," I continue, "and the one for you, Jeff, gave us all pleasure for a long time. It was a little swing that I hung in the doorway to the kitchen. You fit into a little pouch at the bottom, and Mom and I had to get on our knees to push you. But as Chris got a little bigger he'd stand behind you and rock you, gently and for a long time, and you loved it so much."

"You smiled and purred and sucked your thumb and went to sleep," Mrs. Sweetheart adds. "And Chris kept on rocking you for a long time after."

"I know. I've got the picture Dad took."

"You do?" asks Chris.

"I took it to my apartment when I moved."

Chris smiles. I ask him, "Do you remember *your* present?"

Everybody says at the same time, "Butkus!"

"Butkus is still in the attic," his mother says. "Do you want to take him to your apartment?"

"No, I don't need him anymore. Save him though."

"What did you and Mom give each other?" Jeff asks.

"We can't remember," I answer. "But I do remember our first Christmas dinner in Connecticut. I remember it because we almost had nothing to eat at all."

"There was a power failure that afternoon," Mrs. Sweetheart says, "and the stove wouldn't work and I could not even cook."

"I went to the yellow pages and called all the restaurants in town. They were all closed for the holiday. Those were the olden days. There were no Taco Bells or McDonalds on the Old Post Road in those days. But there was a Chinese restaurant open in Portchester, and they agreed to do take-out if I could come and get it."

"Just as I opened the door, the power turned on and the Christmas tree lit up. It was magical."

"It was getting dark and we were hungry," their mother says. "And the house was getting cold."

"I wrapped all of you in blankets, then opened the front door to get to the car. A wall of snow blocked my way. It reached the top of the house now. I clawed a tunnel with my hands, and somehow managed to burrow through to the garage. My hands were numb, my fingers daggers of ice! I grabbed the shovel and made a narrow passageway to the road. Three hours passed. I still wasn't there! The sweat running down my neck had turned to ice. You could have skated down my back. Only your hungry faces staring out the window kept me going, kept me alive."

"I thought some teenagers came by and you gave them five bucks to do the driveway," says Chris.

"Let your father tell the story." Mrs. Sweetheart looks at me. "You're my hero. Go on."

"Well, to make a long story short, I brought home our first Christmas dinner on the coldest day in the history of

Connecticut: hot and spicy Hunan turkey, steamed Chinese dumplings, and one fortune cookie."

"Why only one, Dad?"

"Because the four of us were one. Just as I opened the door, the power turned on and the Christmas tree lit up. It was magical. I can still see the bulbs—red and green and blue—softly lighting the room. Jeff was sleeping under the Christmas tree, right next to the stable. And you sat next to him, Chris, watching over him like the little shepherd guarding baby Jesus in his crib. Mrs. Sweetheart hugged me long and hard in the little house on Havemeyer Lane that was big enough for love. I'll always remember that wonderful night."

"How was the food, Mom?"

"Perfect."

"And what did the fortune cookie say, Dad?"

"I don't remember."

"Mom?"

"I don't remember either. I only know that it said just the right thing. And I want to say just one thing now. *This*, us together right now, is the best Christmas gift your father and I have ever had. Nothing could be better than this."

"You say that every year, Mom," says Chris.

"And you'll say it next year too," adds Jeff.

"That's the way it is," she answers.

"And that's the story of our first Christmas in Connecticut, 1972," I conclude.

"Thanks, Dad, you told it just right," says Jeff.

"Just the way you always do," adds Chris.

We stop talking and eat our pumpkin pie. It's still warm.

I Had Already Named Him Buddy

Patrick Hannon

I n my house as a child you survived mostly on your wits. It was as simple as that. I was the seventh of nine children and the youngest boy. I came into the world a month early, weighing in at just under four pounds. Father Stack poured water on my tiny head in the middle of the night, satisfied that my tiny soul was now fit for heaven.

My parents named me William Patrick. William was my dad's name and Patrick was his paternal grandfather's. My Aunt Barbara brought me home from the hospital—she likes to remind me even to this day—in a shoebox because I was so puny. (I began to lower a doubtful brow upon that apocryphal yarn when I was eleven or twelve, about the time I doubted just about anything any adult told me.)

Being the runt of the Hannon litter, I surmised quickly that if I had any chance of seeing my sixteenth birthday I had to be cunning. I would never carry the bulk or brawn of my older brothers upon my thin frame, and I would certainly never enjoy the clemency afforded my sisters by virtue of their feminine aspect. No, if I wanted seconds at the dinner table or a new pair of sneakers or an extra hour of playtime well after the sun had set or a day free of fraternal torment, I needed to be smarter than my siblings.

And so, when I was eight years old, in a bold and calculated move, I began to cultivate a relationship with my father that would—I was convinced—be mutually beneficial: He would have a relationship with a son worthy of his name and I would enjoy the kind of status within the clan that would keep me content and unbruised.

God breaks through in our lives in ways we could never imagine or anticipate.

As it turned out, this rather devious and selfish plan only served to illustrate the profound truth articulated once long ago by Thomas Aquinas that grace builds on nature (that is, that God breaks through in our lives in ways we could never imagine or anticipate). My simple human desire to survive in the Darwinian jungle of the Hannon household (and—well, all right—my hope that somehow I would become my dad's favorite) brought me closer to a man I was even a little afraid of, but a man, nonetheless, whom I wanted to become when I grew up.

This convoluted strategy culminated on my eighth Christmas in a gift clumsily wrapped in the Sunday funnies, a gift—as I was to discover only years later—that changed the entire direction of my life.

I suppose my family was not unlike most families when it came to Christmas presents. The rule was a simple one: Ask for everything and hope for half. I still have this scene in my head—scripted in my teen years—of my parents late at night in bed going over the list of all the things we crass materialists masquerading as their nine children had pleaded for that day: "Well," Mom would chime in first, "Brian wants a motor scooter, Jack will be catatonic if he doesn't get that damned BB gun, and where in the hell are we going to get three E-Z Bake Ovens?" (My mother, a saint, could nonetheless cuss like a sailor!) "Sally wants a pony, Greg is dead set on that portable Magnavox television set he saw in the window at Andy's TV and Appliance, and Pat is still begging for a puppy."

Dad would reply: "Hmmm?"

"Bill, are you listening? I've done the math, sweetheart, and I just don't see how we're going to manage this year unless you get a second job. Maybe you can deliver the morning paper with the boys."

Dad: "Hmmm?"

(This is where my fantasy morphs into a ridiculous tableau of my father on a rickety bike careening down darkened streets at six in the morning, chucking papers onto roofs and into rose bushes, hating every minute of it but doing it anyway because, well, darn it, he loves his kids.)

I was serious about the puppy though. Johnny Bigelow down the street got a Black Lab the previous Christmas and named him Sarge, and his dad was only a heart surgeon. Here was my dad—the Atticus Finch of Castro Valley, a guy with three suits, a GTO Pontiac convertible, his own office and a secretary. He could certainly afford to buy me a dog. After all, I *was* his namesake and I *was* working on becoming his favorite.

My parents were assaulted daily with Christmas pleadings from my brothers and sisters, and I knew it was getting them nowhere. I can still remember actually seeing my mom's eyes glaze over as she stirred a pot on the stove one night, her brood begging for attention as Christmas Day drew perilously close. God only knows the serene and silent place to which she retreated that evening, but I'm pretty sure it wasn't some spiritual shopping mall.

> My father didn't so much read books as consume them voraciously. On his bedstand always rested a stack of six or seven books, and these were replenished regularly.

Me? I kept to my game plan. I hung out with Dad. I sneaked into his bathroom while he was shaving in the morning and stole a few splashes of his after-shave. I stopped by his office after school just to say hi, and sometimes I waited an hour in his law library until he was finished for the day just to catch a ride home with him. I sat with Dad in the living room at six and watched the evening news and cursed the liberal Democrats in Congress with contempt equal to his own. And almost every night before I went to bed, I lay next to him in his bed and read my book as he read his.

Quite possibly the earliest memory I have of my father is seeing him in bed—under the covers, stripped to his underwear, his black framed prescription glasses pushed up above his forehead. And he is always reading. Apparently, Dad lived by the adage—coined years later by my brother Brian and me at a tavern in San Jose after spending an hour talking about all the books we were reading—"so many books, so little time."

My father didn't so much read books as consume them voraciously. On his bedstand always rested a stack of six or seven books, and these were replenished regularly. The breadth of books he read fascinated me to no end: a biography of Hitler, a Hemingway novel, a book on modern farming techniques, the private journal of Dag Hammarskjold, Shakespeare's *Othello*. Thumbing through their pages, I got a glimpse of hidden, remote worlds begging to be explored, jungles destined to be tamed.

This seemingly magically self-replenishing tower of books by my father's bed helped me partially understand, even at the tender age of eight—how he was able to graduate at the top of his class in law school having never earned his bachelor's degree.

So most nights I scaled my parents' bed, careful not to

drop the book I was carrying with me and thereby disturb my father. I'd like to think that if anyone saw my dad and me reclined there in similar reading postures, our bellies exposed, our lips surreptitiously moving to the lines of words, they would have had a hard time discerning where I ended and my father began.

Years later I came upon this description of the two main characters in one of Flannery O'Conner's stories, "The Artificial Nigger": "They were grandfather and grandson but they looked enough alike to be brothers and brothers not too far apart in age, for Mr. Head had a youthful expression by daylight, while the boy's look was ancient." When I read those words, I thought of the nights I spent with my father, reading together in silence.

But at the time, it was all about the puppy. I was convinced that I had outsmarted my siblings and would on Christmas morning be bathed with the sloppy tongue of the floppy-eared dog I first saw at the pet store two months before. I had already secretly named him "Buddy" and made him my own. I bet I had read at least twenty books with my father during that secret autumn/winter campaign to win his admiration and favor. All that remained for me to do was feign a believable look of surprise and give heartfelt hugs of gratitude when Buddy came bouncing out of the box on Christmas.

When I got out of bed that morning, my first, frantic thought was that Buddy was dead. Not one package or present wrapped tightly in colored paper under or around the blue spruce that morning had holes punched into it through which my puppy might breath fresh air. There was no sound of whimpering or barking. 'My God,' I thought, 'they killed Buddy!' I allowed myself a few moments of stunned desperation before I acknowledged the cold and mocking truth while peals of laughter and delight echoed in our living room as my brothers and sisters became increasingly overwhelmed by the sheer magnitude of their Christmas booty: My campaign had failed; I wasn't getting Buddy.

'My God,' I thought, 'they killed Buddy!'

Dad must have noticed the clouds of disappointment gathering upon my horizon, for he reached down for a package that had been tucked away in the back and said in his faux Santa voice, "Well, well, well. This one must be for Pat!"

Suddenly, I experienced a flicker of hope. A primordial force that seemed to draw its breath from God Himself illuminated my darkened heart. For at least a few seconds, the thought that a puppy might yet still be delivered into my trembling hands was resurrected.

But what I had in my hands was a small package wrapped in Sunday comics, fastened with generous swatches of scotch tape. It had been passed from brother to sister to brother with disinterested hands and dropped on my lap. If it was a puppy, it was a dead puppy; that was for sure. I sadly tore through the wrapping paper, lifted the lid on the box, and dug through the crinkled tissue paper.

It was a book. *The Illustrated History of the World War* by Thomas Herbert, to be exact. It was a first edition copy published by Pictoral Publishing Company of Chicago, Illinois, in 1919. It was beaten up and grungy and the print was too small. It did have pictures and it was about a war—two redeeming qualities no doubt—but I was supremely disappointed. It served me right I thought. My secret little plan had backfired completely. Of course I would get a book! What else could my father have concluded that I really wanted, seeing me next to him nearly every night with my face buried in a book? He knew that I was a boy after his own heart, destined to be a lover of books and literature, just like my old man. But I was an eight-year-old boy, and all I wanted was a puppy for Christmas.

My dad had received straight A's in reading and literature, I noticed, and straight B minuses in morals and manners (a discrepancy I was able to enjoy only much later in life).

"Look inside," my father nudged. "I detected a tone of secret pride in his voice, as if he were talking not so much to his son as he was a soulmate of sorts. Maybe there was a sales slip to the pet store. Maybe Buddy would be mine after all.

There, tucked away in my books pages, was a small yellow card. Upon further inspection I discovered that it was my father's second grade report card. His teacher, Miss

Joanna Sullivan, and his principal, Mr. Jerome Keefer, had seen fit to promote my father to the third grade at Tulelake Grade School on May 26, 1936. My dad had received straight A's in reading and literature, I noticed, and straight B minuses in morals and manners (a discrepancy I was able to enjoy only much later in life).

That Christmas morning, however, this revelation of my father's humanity was cold comfort. Unjustly denied the puppy I thought I had so richly deserved, I shoved my new old book (with its priceless momento of my dad that was absolutely worthless to me at the time) onto the shelf in my closet. Like Coleridge's ancient mariner, I drew consolation from my humiliating defeat only by admitting that though I was a sadder boy that day I was also much wiser.

My father died years later of a sudden heart attack a month before my twenty-sixth birthday. I remember lying awake all night after receiving the phone call. As darkness finally surrendered to the early morning light, I was desperately coaxing from my memory those significant moments in my life that I had shared with him.

The most recent (and unsuspected last) had been after I had taken my first vows in the Congregation of the Holy Cross at our novitiate in Colorado that previous July. My mom and dad were driving me back to Notre Dame in Indiana, and just outside of Marysville, Kansas, my dad got pulled over for speeding. We had been coasting at around ninety and enjoying every minute of it.

'I don't think he actually paid the ticket before he died,' I remember thinking as I finished my memory tour and reached to turn off the light on my bedstand. Then I saw them.

There on my bedstand stood a stack of six or seven books in various stages of consumption. I chuckled aloud as I recalled that dusty memory of my eighth Christmas, when my father gave me a book instead of a puppy.

There on my bedstand stood a stack of six or seven books in various stages of consumption. I chuckled aloud as I recalled that dusty memory of my eighth Christmas, when my father gave me a book instead of a puppy. I went to my closet that very moment and retrieved that book from a storage box. I looked at it again, as if for the first time. I saw now that originally the book had belonged to my namesake, my great-grandfather Patrick Hannon, who died in 1930. My hunch, given my father's second grade report card stashed within its pages, was that *Dad's father* must have given *his father's* book to Dad right around the time of Dad's eighth Christmas.

I have to admit that I had spent the years thinking that my father and I—despite our shared name, rare blood type and southpaw orientation—were irreconcilably different. I had become annoyingly liberal in my politics, passionate about things to which my father gave scant attention, and irritated by his introverted, homebody predilections. I had always loved him and respected him deeply, but there always seemed to be an emotional gully that kept us too often at arm's length from each other.

That early morning of his death, I was blessed to have in my closet a clear and incontrovertible reminder of Dad's love for me—going all the way back to when I was eight and thought that a puppy would make me happy for life. His book and report card were now two of my most precious possessions.

That much was clear. But an even deeper truth dawned on me that morning. I had, in a very real sense, become the man I always wanted to be—not a man who was my father exactly but someone who shares his love for books, for reading, for the literary adventure. That is a gift even better than a puppy with floppy ears.

I read books because I love stories. I read books because someone else has seen something or felt something or thought something or imagined something that maybe I haven't...and I want to know what that something is. I read books because they help me to see the world with more truthful eyes. I read books because it is another way to engage in thoughtful and passionate conversation, whether it is with a fictional character, a historical person long gone to God, or a writer who has something desperate to say. I read because deep and abiding questions always surface in whatever book I attempt to conquer, and those questions almost always bring me to God in prayer. My father gave me all that with that one gift on that one Christmas so long ago.

Five Golden Days

Delle Chatman

It had been a heartbreaking year, 1980.

I had turned thirty the year before—that dreaded age when I knew for certain that I could no longer trust myself. I had intoned that mantra of the 1960s, "Don't trust anyone over thirty" dozens of times, but now I was that purveyor of establishment principles, that corporate sell-out, that (gulp!) adult Delle. I wasn't ready. I wasn't nearly ready. But ready or not, in 1980 I knew for certain all my mistakes were my own and not my parents'. I was responsible, completely and irrevocably independent, and had declared as much early in the year when I decided for the very last time that I absolutely could not, would not, go into my father's business. If life was going to be a mess, then it would darn well be my mess and not a mess painted over with position and money and prestige. I drew my let-me-live-as-an-artist line in the sand in 1980, but that short flight of euphoria ended as soon as the next rent check came due. Santa Monica's gray waves washed that line in the sand out to sea and left my feet wet and cold, my sense of direction waterlogged, and my resolve soggy.

1980 exhausted me with highs and lows.

I ended a seven-year relationship that had been spiritually destructive and felt a wave of liberation flow through me something like Ibsen's Nora leaving her "Doll's House." The stress of that break-up had shrunk me down to a sweet size six. I learned to dress like a woman instead of a hippie. I turned in my eyeglasses for contacts. I started wearing my hair long, even if it meant buying the extra length. I wanted everything about me to be swinging. The caterpillar grew wings.

> *I wanted everything about me to be swinging. The caterpillar grew wings.*

My first full-length play opened to marvelous reviews with me in one of the leading roles, praised for both the writing and the acting. It was the largest role I'd ever played and the most emotionally mature work I'd ever written. We played to full houses, at least until the theater producer went broke!

My paternal grandmother dropped into town out of the blue that summer and stayed with me for a few days. I hadn't seen her in more than a decade. *Mea culpa, mea culpa, mea maxima culpa.* How had I ignored that fountain of love for so long? How had I let ambition and the quest for a husband push that human treasure to the far edge of my consciousness? How had I allowed my grandmother's love to become a given rather than a gift?

A steep stockpile of guilt threatened to sour the entire visit, until Grandmother kicked the whole thing down with "I kept my eye on you through prayer, Delle." It will never feel like anything other than a cold-blooded shame that I let that much time go by without being in touch with her, but I swallowed my shame and sat at her knee for three days, drinking in her wisdom and warmth, just as in the old days.

She had always been my all-time favorite relative. All those soft-bosomed hugs. All those delicious meals she folded into Mom's so-so repertoire when she came to visit. All those nights we lay awake together in my bed, talking about everything under the sun. All those laughs we had. She told me I was "rotten to the core" and I was. She told me to "Stay sweet!" even though she knew I wouldn't/couldn't/hadn't. When she suddenly plunked back into my life, the Hollywood lifestyle that had consumed every ounce of my devotion found a familial foundation that grounded me in reality again. I was reminded of a world far beyond the poolside, studio-bound culture of ambition and fame.

Unfortunately, Grandmother's reminder of what truly mattered in life had not arrived in time to prevent me from sacrificing one of God's unborn souls in order to continue my assault on the crystal palace of success unencumbered by a mother's responsibilities. Having adopted a blithe agnosticism while in college, I had committed my darkest sin earlier in 1980. Expediency and ambition collided with a crippled conscience, and a tiny life was snuffed out in the pile-up—because somewhere along the road to that intersection, without ever realizing it, I had sold my soul. Grandmother had heard all about it from her son, my father, and she had wanted to intercede with an offer of help and support such as only she could have given. But my father had prevented her, for he believed that the question of whether or not to abort the life growing inside me needed to be *my* decision.

I returned to God's flock severely wounded, confused, and weak beyond words. As the year drew to a close, I felt lost, found, and then lost again.

And so it was. Sequestered in anguished, bell jar isolation, I made the most momentous and tragic decision of my life.

To this day, I wonder what I might have done if only Grandmother....

As God would have it, my child's rejected little spirit became the conduit for my own redemption, making its own afterlife so real to me that I had to acknowledge God and love as the eternal bridge between life and death. But I returned to God's flock severely wounded, confused, and weak beyond words. As the year drew to a close, I felt lost, found, and then lost again.

When 1980 started wrapping itself up, I realized that none

of my good news had been good enough or big enough or lasting enough to fill the chasm I had recently discovered within my own soul. With the seven-year affair behind me, I had no warm cuddly to "hug up on" through the holidays. Since my parents' divorce was new and fresh, neither of them seemed like good, uplifting holiday company.

My grandmother had been the life preserver God had tossed out onto my stormy waves that year, so I got it in my head that I would spend five days around Christmas in the comfort zone of her house. I would carry my tattered, battered heart, my confused future, my wobbly ego, and my newly resurrected but desperately immature faith down to the countrified suburbs of Little Rock, Arkansas. I planned to sleep once again in that wonderful tiny bedroom between Grandmother's bedroom in the back of the house and Daddy James' bedroom up front. I would enter the house that had been my castle of love in my childhood, where the biggest dangers were the wasps that found their way past the screens in summer time. I would hide under my grandmother's wings for Christmas.

I wanted to watch Grandmother shuffle around the kitchen making cornbread and greens, dirtying every pot in the house in the process. I would wash the pots after her, I thought. I would learn the recipes at last; I would see how big a pinch of this or that made all the difference. I would learn all the culinary secrets my mother had withheld all the years of my childhood, as though to let me see her work was tantamount to discovering the man behind the curtain in the Oz palace. I just knew that Grandmother would let me watch over her shoulder. If anyone could make a cook out of me, she would. Or so I hoped.

So on December 23rd, I left the sunny, smoggy comfort of Los Angeles for the cool, gray woods and dusty back roads of Panky, Arkansas.

When Grandmother had visited me earlier that year in Los Angeles, she and I had hopped over the decade-wide gap in our relationship and picked up where we had left off—as warm and funny and soft and close as ever. But I hadn't been in Arkansas in twenty years. Little Rock had changed, sprawling out to meet what had been backwoods when last I visited. Now instead of being a magical rural wonderland where kids went barefoot, climbed trees and waded across narrow streams, Panky was just one more poor neighborhood on the grimy outskirts of a large but struggling big city, a suburb no one felt compelled to gentrify.

I saw my father's journey out of this life into the "Entrepreneur of the Year" award-winning prosperity as the great escape it most certainly had been.

As the taxi turned off the two-lane highway onto the gravel road that led to Grandmother's house, another reality check blossomed in my consciousness.

I understood yet again what humble roots my father and mother had sprung from. I realized afresh how great an achievement my parents' college education had been. I saw my father's journey out of this life into the "Entrepreneur of the Year" award-winning prosperity as the Herculean accomplishment, the great escape it most certainly had been.

How time magnifies the memories it tucks away for storage. This house that had loomed before me as a ten-year-old, every bit the largest, most luxurious domicile I'd ever beheld, now appeared to have shrunk to a shanty of itself. My one-bedroom apartment in Los Angeles, though smaller in square footage, actually felt more spacious than the humble abode my grandfather had built with his own hands half a century before—on a railroad porter's salary, no less.

The last time I'd seen my grandparents' home, sunflowers taller than me had been blooming in the front yard, most of them planted inside the plugged up water well that was no longer needed once running water and modern plumbing had been installed. The aroma of gladiolas and roses, whippoorwills and freshly mowed grass used to make my head swim. Big, fat bumblebees had buzzed everywhere, and I remembered the constant drone of cicadas, from dewy morning to gentle night (when the crickets took up the evening shift). Grandmother had always seemed to be waist deep in the vegetable garden, under a straw hat and her perfect pageboy hairstyle, not a strand of gray in it. Or she would be in the kitchen cooking or canning or baking up whatever she'd harvested that day—along with Daddy

James' fresh catch or the chicken deemed ripe for execution and consumption.

On December 23, 1980, however, I learned what cruel time could do to a fragile paradise like the one my grandparents had created for themselves. The house was falling apart, and the great big shade tree that had been such a source of comfort and pride had been cut off at an unceremonious height of four feet. Why? Because the wisteria vine that had decorated it so elegantly all those years ago had become as big and thick as a tree trunk itself and had warped the tree's trunk so dramatically that it finally leaned too dangerously toward the roof. Rather than lose the house, Daddy James had sawed off both vine and tree at once. They had grown together and then died together to keep from crushing the house they had blessed with shade through all those hot Arkansas summers. I knew looking at their remains that I was definitely no longer a child, no longer a teen, no longer an irresponsible twenty-something. Everything that I could call my "youth" was now behind me, dead, finished before I was ready to let go of it, cut down like the wisteria and the evergreen.

> *Everything that I could call my "youth" was now behind me, dead, finished before I was ready to let go of it, cut down like the wisteria and the evergreen.*

Grandmother must have read the shock and exhaustion on my face when I arrived, because she fed me some of last night's leftovers and rushed me off to bed in the prettiest, gentlest, warmest room I had ever known. That guest-room—between her world and her husband's—always charmed me with its deep peach walls and its chenille bedspread of the softest cotton ever woven to suit a practical purpose. It couldn't have been the same spread I had grown up with. That would have made the thing over a quarter century old. But where—in this modern age of polyester-filled comforters and crispy synthetic but resolutely matching pillow shams—where, oh, where had Grandmother found another bedspread just like that chenille beauty I had always cherished? And how had she kept that room precisely the same as it always was, when so much else around the place had changed?

These were riddles I was unlikely to solve that night, for I crashed and burned without even unpacking, promising myself I'd ask all my questions tomorrow and that Grandmother would have all the answers.

I spent Christmas Eve adjusting my fantasy to fit the reality. Since Grandmother no longer got up with the chickens, I fixed breakfast and carried it into her room, realizing for the first time that she and her husband had probably been living their sexually chaste lifestyle for decades. My grandfather, whom we had always called "Daddy James," resided in the front of the house. Grandmother slept in the larger bedroom off the kitchen, a room with its own fireplace and two large windows that looked out onto the back yard. Clearly, her room had been built as the family room, but it had become a bedroom once their marriage reached its current "understanding." They had both obviously become comfortable within the narrow parameters of the arrangement. They were courteous, even friendly with each other, and that made it easy for me fall into a similar ease with both of them.

I learned that romantic heartache can be a congenital condition, visited upon generation after generation unless aggressive healing measures are applied.

It was too cold to take a walk through the woods, this spoiled Los Angelina decided, so I settled down with a cup of tea and watched Daddy James bring a gigantic log into Grandmother's room on a hand truck. I had never seen anyone feed such a mammoth into a fireplace before, but he rolled it into the back of the fireplace, built a fire in front of it, and assured me that it would burn through the entire day. He was right.

I watched the logs in front of the backlog turn to ash, but that big round beauty melted ever so slowly. When Daddy James had left to do whatever he did with his days after retirement, I settled down to unburden myself of a year's worth of emotional chaos and spiritual confusion. There would be no Christmas tree—for neither Grandmother nor Daddy James had the strength or the desire to hunt down ornaments let alone to put them up and take them down. But there were two large, aging red candles on the mantelpiece above the fireplace, which I lit after lunch and blew out every evening. They were our only Christmas decorations…and they were the silent, steady witnesses to a feast of sharing that took me four days to consume.

I learned how Grandmother's marriage had become what it was.

I learned why she didn't leave.

I learned why Daddy James didn't leave.

I learned how faith had given my grandmother the will to forgive and how it had given my grandfather the will to change.

I learned that romantic heartache can be a congenital condition, visited upon generation after generation unless aggressive healing measures are applied, and I came to believe that—given my parents' divorce—it was up to my brothers and me to turn the tide around for our tribe.

Listening to my grandmother's life story, I learned how insignificant my ambitions and lusts were. I suddenly recognized the courage it takes to diffuse economic hardship with compassion, the strength of character needed to minimize the oppression of racism by focusing on a merciful God. In my grandmother, I saw a depth of faith that embraced God as Someone as real and dear as the most wayward of granddaughters.

I took those grace-filled presents home with me a couple days after Christmas.

And I've been opening them ever since.

The Frog
in the Manger

Fredric Hang

few years ago, my mother unearthed an old black and white photograph. It was taken on Christmas Eve, 1956. I stood as a six-year-old boy in front of an aluminum tree, wearing a goofy grin from cheek to cheek, holding a large stuffed frog. The frog was sporting a spiffy bow tie, a top hat, and a smile almost as silly as mine.

There are some childhood gifts you never forget. The plastic Noah's ark with over fifty pairs of animals never ceased to flood my imagination. My first Etch-A-Sketch set lasted well into my teens. The wind-up music box that played "The Farmer in the Dell" drove my sisters crazy for years—I *loved* that. Oh, and I'll always remember the miniature tool shop my grandfather made with meticulous detail, lots of love, and all kinds of moving parts.

But I have to admit that I had no recollection of that frog in my mother's picture, which is really strange in light of my adult obsession with frogs.

Every Christmas for the past several years, I have placed a tiny ceramic frog in my nativity scene. But to understand why, you have to know how the whole frog thing got started.

I was a young Catholic priest in the early 1980s, regularly presiding at a children's liturgy in a parish in Chicago. This served as a refreshing change of pace from my professional work as a homiletics professor at a large, urban theological union. I enjoyed the kids' spontaneity, their unexpected questions, and their uninhibited critique of my preaching.

> I cannot tell you how many times the kids and I talked about God loving us "warts and all."

One Christmas, a woman who regularly attended these liturgies made what she called a "story stole" for me. On it she'd sewn a little boy and girl, a sunburst, a tree, a flower…and a frog. I used to put the stole on during story time with the children after the Gospel, and it was the frog that always seemed to capture the most attention. I cannot tell you how many times the kids and I talked about God loving us "warts and all" or about how—even when we're feeling like an ugly toad—there is always a prince or princess inside somewhere, waiting to come out like Lazarus from the tomb. Over time, the children began associating "Father Fred" with the frog.

Because of a new assignment, the time came for me to end my participation in these children's liturgies. At my final one, the children presented me with a small ceramic frog. I kept it on my office desk as a treasured memento of that happy time. It soon begot others.

"Oh Father, I see ya like frogs?" one man said, noticing the frog on my desk. "My wife makes 'em outta macramé...I'll get one for ya." Someone gave me a frog quilt, another a frog robe (made of glow-in-the-dark material). One person brought me an exquisite crystal frog from Italy. I got plenty of Kermit dolls and figurines, of course, and even a *coquí* with a straw hat from Puerto Rico. I received big frogs, small frogs, frogs made from every material imaginable. I have received over 250 frogs of various kinds, including enough frog ornaments to trim an entire Christmas tree each year.

As the 1980s came to an end, my life took some sharp turns. First, there was facing up to my alcoholism. Drinking can be a slow, sneaky insidious disease. Years of dependency on it finally caught up with me. I came to admit I was powerless to overcome my drinking by myself and sought help. Treatment for alcoholism and the powerful spirituality of the twelve steps, however, led to facing even more truths about myself. The hardest, without a doubt, was accepting my sexual orientation.

As a celibate priest for over sixteen years, it had really

seemed unimportant for me to come to grips with "whom" I was sexually attracted to, since I had no intention of pursuing it anyway. And homosexuality was certainly not something we priests talked about in those days.

But my sexual orientation was *not* deemed insignificant to my counselors and spiritual directors. They had the wisdom to know that we Christians all come to the Lord and serve the Lord as we are—in all our mystery and complexity. They resolutely refused to let me ignore this important part of myself, which I would have much preferred to bury in scotch and work.

Finally, the time came for me to practice what I had preached to those children years before.

Finally, the time came for me to practice what I had preached to those children years before. Did I really believe that God loves me "as I am?" Did I believe that there was a "prince inside me somewhere" waiting to come out? Did I believe that what I was experiencing was not a curse but a gift from God to keep me both humble and compassionate?

With recovery, I no longer depended on alcohol to numb my feelings, especially those around my sexuality. I had to rely more and more on God for direction with what to do with this part of myself that I had spent most of my life ignoring and denying. I had some decisions to make. One of them was to begin to be honest with myself and with my family and friends. Another was to take a long and thoughtful leave from the priesthood and religious life.

I will never forget my mother's response to all of this. Just before Christmas during my leave, while I was in a treatment program for my addiction to alcohol, she came to visit. In that one afternoon of wonderful openness and honesty between us, she found out that I was a recovering alcoholic, gay, and leaving the priesthood—all at the same time.

My mom is a woman of few words. After some quiet tears, she embraced me and then handed me a gift she had bought at the hospital gift shop before she came up to see me. It was a huge stuffed frog! This one had a little red knapsack on its back. In the knapsack was a handwritten note from Mom: "I love you, warts and all."

During that period and ever since as a lay person, leaving the Church has never seemed a viable option for me. I am one of those die-hard "once a Catholic, always a Catholic" kind of folk. I'd be less than honest, however, if I told you finding my new place in the Church has been easy. But somehow the gifts of all those frogs over the years has made things more tolerable and helped me persevere.

On a silent night long ago, a little baby was born. Not in a palace, but in a stable. Who knows why God chose such common surroundings to become flesh? But I figure that if cows and mules and sheep and camels could find their way there, maybe a frog did too.

As I mentioned, each year I now place that small ceramic frog the children gave me among the flowing Fontanini figurines in my nativity set. It is jarring at first, with its odd-green color and unexpected shape, and more than a few of my friends have asked, "What is a frog doing in the manger?"

I just let them wonder.

Big Harriett Herself, in Open-Toed Platform Heels, Walking Bosco and Bismark

Carol DeChant

atholic children in the 1940s and 1950s were alternately ignored and admonished by adults who didn't much like kids but strived to have lots of them. Children should be seen and not heard, sit still, be quiet, don't cry, act ladylike, be a little man—it was as if our parents were trying to deny us our very childlike nature.

Yet everyone wanted a big family, and those who fell drastically short of that goal were pitied. My girlfriend Mary Ellen once took a bratty vengeance on Peter Broderick's mother (Peter was that anomaly, the Only Child) after Mrs. Broderick chased her out of their yard. "You're not a good Catholic, because you only have one child," Mary Ellen (the eldest of six) yelled back at Peter's mom.

"The *Virgin Mary* only had one child," Mrs. B. replied.

The Blessed Virgin aside, the only fate worse than an only child was no child. Momma constantly reminded Kathleen, Little Harriett, and me that the elderly Protestant couple next door had never had children. We understood this to mean that they were clueless about what kids were really like—and we were not to enlighten them. Aunt Harriett (a.k.a. Big Harriett) never had children either. Yet I was eight years old when I got my best Christmas gift ever, and she gave it to me.

I don't know how Big Harriett got the idea to give a camera to a kid my age. Taking pictures was an adult activity then. Buying and developing film cost good money (which didn't grow on trees, our parents would remind us) far beyond what was entrusted to children in that era. That Brownie Hawkeye, along with little bulbs to screw into its silver flash attachment—all in a tan leather carrying case—was a lavish gift for a young girl.

In a world where being a child was a tedious and demanding business, the camera became my currency for occasional forays into adult territory.

I loved it and all that it implied about her confidence in me. For in a world where being a child was a tedious and demanding business, the camera became my currency for occasional forays into adult territory. My parents let me walk to Karr's Drugstore and buy supplies whenever I wanted to, and I didn't squander film. I'd walk around the neighborhood for days with my loaded camera, looking for shots. It took me a long time to use a roll.

When I'd take it to the drug store to be developed, an elderly clerk named Raleigh became curious, and he began to look at my prints when they came back from the processor. I'd go in to pick them up, and Raleigh would evaluate my work, "You got some good ones this time," or "You moved the camera on some of these." Once he asked why I'd taken several shots of a dead bird, a nearly unrecognizable muddy lump shot in black and white. I was unable to explain myself, but I sensed that Raleigh respected my decision to experiment. I had never been of interest to an adult outside of our family before, and Raleigh's attention gave my photography a significance beyond anything else I'd ever done.

Before long, the camera earned me another perk among the adults: I was becoming the family chronicler. Our albums from that time on would not exist without all the photos I took. "Look here," we would say...

"...there's Aunt Betsey. Remember when she wore this hat—that veil was the latest style then—to that ladies' luncheon? And when the flowers on the table triggered her allergy, Aunt Betsey blew her nose, forgetting all about the veil, which pulled the hat down over her face? And how she had to extricate herself from that disgusting mess, just as Lola Ferguson was finishing a dramatic recitation?"

"...that's the folks standing in front of our DeSoto."

"…and this is Grandma and Grandpa playing bridge with Momma and Aunt Hilda. Remember how noisy they'd get after each hand, trying to out-yell each other about who should have bid what?"

"…and here we are in front of the Nash Rambler."

"…that's Little Harriett on the dock at Lake Okoboji, reading *True Confessions*. (No, that was *not* a Catholic magazine).

"…and this is Grandpa and Uncle Clayton, waving their El Productos, debating whether Dewey lost because voters don't trust a man with a mustache or if 'Give-'em-hell Harry' Truman made him seem weak."

"…and this one is the folks again, by the Valiant."

"…and here's Big Harriett herself, in those open-toed platform heels she always wore, walking Bosco and Bismark."

I am missing from all of these photos, of course. My absenteeism was inevitable, given my role as the picture-taker, and intentional, for other reasons. I'm still reminded of just how successful my disappearing act was, like when I recently visited two elderly relatives in Iowa nursing homes. When I left Uncle Herb, he said, "Goodbye, Kathleen." When I left Cousin Eddie, he said, "Goodbye, Harriett." I was not surprised to find myself the first one of the three of us sisters blacked-out during the eclipse of their long term memory.

Early on, we middle children find ourselves in that twilight zone between alpha and omega, where no one knows your name. By the time I got my camera, I saw advantages to being stationed there.

I had already begun the growth spurt that would end in seventh grade with me at five-foot-ten, towering over my classmates and teachers too. My childhood longing was for my ever-visible self to be unnoticed.

In those days, hiding behind the camera gave me an excuse never to be in front of it.

Confronting my gawky reflection in mirrors made back-to-school shopping a humiliating ritual. Dresses were not designed for a long-waisted girl who was taller sitting down than most people were standing up. Buster Brown and his pooch didn't inhabit shoes that fit me. Only old-lady styles and nun shoes came in size nine-and-a-half.

In those days, hiding behind the camera gave me an excuse never to be in front of it. I became like my comic-book hero, Invisible Scarlet O'Neil, a justice-enforcer with the ability to mingle unseen among unsuspecting guilty parties. (We readers knew that Scarlet had tapped into her power whenever she became a shadow of her former self.)

In junior high, I announced that I was going to become a real photographer when I grew up, a decision prompted by an assignment to write a career book. The project required me to interview someone in my chosen field. George Yates, the head of photography at the *Des Moines Register* and *Tribune* newspapers, a Brit who learned his trade in the Royal Air Force during World War I, said yes. I was thrilled just to walk through the newsroom to get to his office, passing desks marked with the names of columnists I saw every day in the papers.

I was doing more than merely capturing our lives on film. I was editing them too.

Even more exciting was that Mr. Yates took me seriously enough to share knowledge that no other adult would have told a kid back then. He said that he hired "B" students, because "A" students were conformists who lack the daring that photography often calls for. His first big assignment, he explained, was to shoot the coronation of King George VI in Westminster Abbey—where taking photos was forbidden. Mr. Yates acquired a choir robe, then marched in with the singers, hiding his tiny camera until they reached the sanctuary. Like Scarlet O'Neil, Mr. Yates had disappeared to do his work. He told me those shots he took "under cover" launched his career.

Shortly after that, my father let me use his 16mm Revere movie camera and a 35mm Leica, and he was pleased that I took them out more than he did. By then, I was doing more than merely capturing our lives on film. I was editing them too. Family albums from previous generations have photos of people in their coffins, recognizing death as a family milestone along with graduations, weddings and First Communions. In the albums I put together, however, death (like divorce) is suggested only by the figures suddenly missing from our archives. Nor are there photos of the hidden bottle, the pink slip being awarded, or faces ravaged by disease, unkempt because of depression, or traumatized by war. We stand there, mostly young and hopeful, in dress-up clothes, tilting the birthday cake before the knife is applied, saying "cheese." We are preserved always leaving for the dance, never returning from it.

By choosing what to document—and what not to—I unearthed my special power as our generation's story-teller, too young then to understand that the stories families conceal have a power of their own. Grandma and Grandpa Graney once took chairs out into the yard so the family could be photographed in front of the farmhouse. Turn a page, and the farm disappears forever as a backdrop. But the nightmare of losing the farm rippled down through the generations, haunting Graney descendants who never even saw it.

I met Mr. Yates again in my junior year at Drake University, where he was teaching photojournalism. He designed a night class to simulate actual work on a newspaper. Students who had cars were partnered with those of us who didn't, and once a week each duo drew a different assignment from a hat. We had to return in two hours and give Mr. Yates our exposed film, which he developed for us at the *Tribune*.

One Tuesday evening, my partner Dick Hatfield, a Korean War vet, reached into the assignment hat and pulled out: "Illustrate the weather." We drove around town with the sun setting and our desperation rising. It was clear and it was dark and the clock was ticking. Where could we find any "weather"? Finally, we came upon the minor league ballpark and saw that the Des Moines Bruins were playing a game under the lights. The image of a perfect night in spring.

> *When I handed in my film that night, I felt like a real photographer for the first time.*

We were wondering how to get good shots without telephoto lenses when Hatfield spotted an opening in the wooden fence behind right field. We crawled through, then quickly got to work shooting the fielders and the nearest spectators until both of us had finished our rolls. To our surprise, no one chased us out. When I handed in my film that night, I felt like a real photographer for the first time, worthy of a perfect "B" from Mr. Yates.

By now, however, supergirls had fallen on hard times.

Newspaper editors had decided female heroes were unsuited to the 1950s, so Invisible Scarlet O'Neil's career changed drastically. No longer able to become suddenly invisible by pressing a nerve in her wrist, Scarlet tried life as a cowgirl, with a (male) sidekick. Then her popularity faded completely. Once she had lost her nerve, just plain Scarlet O'Neil disappeared forever.

Within the decade, my old life had vanished too. After ten years as a full time wife and mother, I needed to get a job. My camera then, a Bell and Howell 35mm, gave me a leg up in getting free lance writing assignments. I was never a professional-caliber photographer, but I'd learned to shoot a full roll for every story to get at least one or two usable pictures. Once again, my camera became my passport to enter foreign territory…and to do so inconspicuously.

That early gift from Aunt Harriett has inspired my own holiday giving. As the last survivors of their generation, my parents have inherited all of their families' albums, with some photos dating back to Lincoln's presidency. At Christmastime, I make prints of ancestor portraits and send them to my cousins. Among the first sent to my Graney cousins was of a young Big Harriett, her flamboyant red hair (our memory supplies the tint) mostly covered by a flapper-era cloche.

Harriett had cared for my grandparents for many years and so married too late in life to have children. Unfamiliar with kids as she was, she didn't know any better than to give me something that was not (as we say today) age-appropriate. Thank goodness.

The Brownie Hawkeye is long gone, but I still have its leather case. I keep my Nikon in it now. It sits on a shelf in the bedroom, reminding me that the greatest gifts I've ever received have been ones I didn't even know I wanted. It's a relic of early years of reverence, of that time when looking through a lens allowed me to see creation anew, when family occasions and Karr's drug store were church, when strangers came forth to guide me and share my wonder, of summer days on the front porch pasting my photos in albums— preserving what were to become our family's sacred images.

Her gift freed me from the confines of my own childhood, and its enchantment has abounded throughout my lifetime.

My aunt never knew any of this, nor did she anticipate the regenerative power of her Christmas present to me. How could she? How can any of us, when we come bearing gifts?

I saw little of Aunt Harriett in the years before her death. Every move I made after college put more miles between us, so we had to rely on Christmas letters to stay in touch. The last time we talked was when she phoned on my wedding day. I was too rattled to say much. I didn't even think to let her know that I had met my groom at a photography exhibit in Chicago.

Over the years, I always meant to tell Harriett that my children were being extensively photographed (always in archival black and white). Her gift freed me from the confines of my own childhood, and its enchantment has abounded throughout my lifetime. She died in 1989, yet I find myself longing to tell her...

...how the shutter-click has always triggered pinpricks of excitement—right from those first days it transported me into adult territory.

...how I'm electrified still, when I've just captured an image of my grandkids that I think their descendants will cherish.

...and especially how, during these moments, I am eight years old again.

The Christmas Kaleidoscope

John Shea

The Christmas tree was a gangly forest fir that had no shape. Branches at the top were long and knobby. One stuck out like E.T.'s finger. At the middle was a waistband of short branches, giving the impression the tree was sucking in its stomach for a Christmas photo. Near the bottom, a branch grew straight down. There were ornaments, tinsel, lights and garlands doing what they could, but no amount of cosmetics could camouflage the gaps or cover the bare stretches. The tree's only virtue was that it was tall, but even that worked against it. Its height left so little room for the angel at the top that her wings were bent against the ceiling. On the whole, it was an over-dressed, underdeveloped fir trying unsuccessfully to pass as a Christmas tree.

When my brother Alex saw it, he took a slow sip of his martini and said, "Now I know why they invented artificial trees."

But the presents were stacked beneath it and we were gathered around it—all my extended family, come from far and near on Christmas Eve (to grandmother's house no less). Each of us was decoratively decked out, but not without a bent wing here or a bare stretch of branch there. The tree was no stranger to our gathering. It fit in. It was one of us. And I like to think it was redeemed by the company it kept.

Malaise is the word, I guess, but I don't care enough to look it up.

However, lately I have not been much company. Some sadness has moved into my heart, like a fog that comes off the sea. You do not notice it until it has engulfed you. It's nothing physical. The doctor looked at blood profiles and x-rays and just shrugged. But I am numb. I cannot muster even a passing pleasure. If you slapped my soul, it wouldn't move. *Malaise* is the word, I guess, but I don't care enough to look it up.

I saw my condition clearly last week. My wife Eleanor and I went to a party at some friends of ours who live in a condominium. We parked in the basement and, as we were waiting for the elevator, there was a sudden noise coming from the storage area. I turned and a clothes rack—one of those carts on wheels that people use to transport cleaning and clothes—was coming toward us, splashing through the puddles left by the snow that had melted off the cars. At the front of the rack was a girl of about ten, hanging on to the vertical pole, leaning forward. She reminded me of Kate Winslet leaning over the front of the Titanic. Someone quite long in the tooth played the Leonardo DiCaprio role. I suspect it was her grandfather. He was pushing the rack from behind and had it going fast enough to lift the long, blondish-brown hair of his granddaughter ever so slightly off her shoulders. Both of them were laughing.

As they sped by, I waved. Then I turned and watched them move down the parking garage until they turned the corner and disappeared. I couldn't get enough of them. As the elevator took us up to the party, I said to myself, "God, I wish I could push that clothes rack."

Eleanor looked at me and said, "What?"

"Nothing," I said. "Nothing, just thinking out loud."

The elevator door opened. The distraction of the party was only a few feet away.

So the scrawny tree was no stranger to my spirit as we all gathered around it, squeezed into the living room, even overflowing into the dining room. It was time to open the presents. We waited as the patriarchs and matriarchs settled into chairs or claimed a section of sofa. The rest of us either stood or found a piece of floor. I plopped down at the back of the room and leaned against the wall. It was a good spot. I could see most of my family and relatives, but they could not see me. I would be able to catch their expressions as they pulled the hidden treasure from the plundered boxes, but I wouldn't have to pretend I was enthusiastic myself.

Without fanfare, the gift giving began. Presents came out from under the tree and were passed along to their rightful recipient. For an hour the room was filled with the sound of tearing paper and laughing, the sound of tearing paper and "ooing," the sound of tearing paper and kissing, the sound of tearing paper and "ahhing," the sound of tearing paper and thanking. Finally, with the floor a bright, undulating sea of torn wrapping paper, a collective exhaustion set in and we sat for a second of silence amid shambles of Christmas giving.

The last present, finger-printed by the people I love, was in my lap... and I couldn't care less.

Then my nephew, who had been playing Santa Claus and handing out the presents with great precision, announced, "The last present goes to Uncle Paul."

I saw it coming toward me, a moderate-sized box with an immoderate bow, being passed along a chain of people from the hand of my nephew to the hand of my grandfather to the hand of my mother to the hand of my sister to the hand of my wife to the hand of my daughter and finally to my own hand. The last present, fingerprinted by the people I love, was in my lap...and I couldn't care less.

I looked for a card or name tag, but I could not find one. Then I looked up and saw that everyone's face was turned toward me in Christmas anticipation. I felt a flush of panic that I was going to be found out, discovered in my secret sadness I could not even name.

I quickly ripped the paper, but got no joy from the sound or feel. Underneath was a naked rectangular box that gave no indication of what was inside. I pulled open the top and felt a slight swoosh of air. Inside was a velvet bag with a gold cord knotting the top. I untied the cord and the velvet bag slid down.

It was a large kaleidoscope. The casing was real wood, a dark stained oak that gave it a polished, handsome look. It came with a stand that made a clear statement: "I am not an ordinary, budget-bin kaleidoscope. I belong in a prominent place, displayed on a table or shelf. I do not deserve the back of the closet and, under no circumstances, should I disappear beneath the bed." This was a gift that took itself seriously.

There wasn't a card in the box either. It was a gift without a giver.

"Who do I have to thank for this?" I asked.

Nobody said anything. Finally, my wife said, "Santa, of course!"

It was as if that word, "Santa," was a signal. People got up immediately and were stirring around—asking about dinner or making themselves another drink. The gift giving was officially over, and I was left alone with my anonymous gift.

My wife came over and, holding her dress down with one hand, sat next to me on the floor. Then she said with infinite gentleness and a touch of wickedness, "Aren't you going to look through the kaleidoscope, Scrooge?"

I laughed despite myself and put it to my eye, monocle fit, and turned it. The technicolor pieces twisted and tumbled into a pattern. It was stunning. I turned it again and the pieces fell into chaos and then stepped festively into a new beauty. I took my time as my eye drank in its pleasure. Then I turned it again. I could not get enough of it.

In my ear, whispering, was the voice of my wife: "It was the closest I could find to a clothes rack."

I put down the kaleidoscope and looked at her. I slid my hand under her hair, resting it on the nape of her neck. Then I flicked my hand and her hair lifted off her shoulders, like a little girl's. It was as if some sudden Christmas wind had rushed through the room, bestowing life on those who needed it.

The Frequent Bald
Statements of Love
We Exchange

Patrick T. Reardon

Christmas gifts are such a loaded thing in our culture. Look at the commercials, read the ads. There's an attitude that the expense and quality of a gift is a measure—no, *the* measure—of love. There's also the implied corollary that if I don't get exactly what I want for Christmas *and* if I don't get a whole lot of "valuable" things, then I'm not loved and Christmas has been a bust. Thus, disappointment with the entire season is virtually guaranteed, beginning in childhood and continuing right through old age.

This is an American illness, one I acknowledge I'm afflicted with. So thinking about the Christmas presents I've received is a complicated exercise for me, as apt to bring up sour memories as joyful ones.

There is one gift, though, that I keep before me all the time. And it's the representative of the type of gift that never disappoints—the gift that always leaves me feeling loved, filled with joy and life, as happy as a lord-a-leaping.

Like many men, I use the top of my dresser as a sort of domestic desk. Here is where I put the letters to be mailed. Here is where I put my keys, coins and wallet when I empty my pockets at night. And here is where I have photos and keepsakes and a Christmas card that I received maybe three years ago from my son David.

Think of it as a hand-made card, although David, who was twelve or thirteen at the time, used the card-making software on our home computer to help create it.

The card's the thing— the universally accepted gift in our family, the one that requires no explanation, apology or justification.

We do that a lot in our family—make greeting cards and thank-you cards and birthday cards with this Print Shop Deluxe software. I like to import images, usually of great works of art or other interesting subjects, from the Internet and fashion my own designs. David and his sister Sarah tend to use the images and designs offered by the software. My wife Cathy doesn't use the computer in this way. She prefers to buy a card at the store and write a long message on the inside. But the card's the thing—the universally accepted gift in our family, the one that requires no explanation, apology or justification.

This particular card from David is a little unusual inasmuch as he supplemented the computer text and imagery with nearly two dozen small Christmas-season stickers.

So, on the front of the card he has the words "Merry Christmas" inside a snowflake border, courtesy of the computer. But then he's added another border of small stickers of mistletoe and candy canes and Christmas tree ornaments. And, in the center, he's put a sticker of a home scene featuring Santa and Mrs. Santa.

A sticker of Santa appears on the back of the card as well, this time sitting in a big chair with a little girl on his lap. There is also a Frosty the Snowman sticker and one of mistletoe. And at the bottom there are the computer-generated words, "Hallmark Collection." (In our family, we like pretending that these homemade cards are store-bought. Often, we'll make up a fictional publishing company, such as Reardon Productions, and add a price—say, $7.95.)

Inside the card, David created another snowflake border and filled much of the space with still more stickers of Santa and candy canes and Christmas stockings. On the right side he used the computer to write this message: *"Dear Dad, I hope you have a wonderful Christmas!! I know you haven't been feeling good for the last couple of days but I hope that changes. I hope you like all the gifts you've got or your getting. I love you so much. Merry Christmas! Love, David Reardon."* And, above his name, he wrote his flowing, distinctive signature in red ink: David J. Reardon.

There are details of that message that I find particularly touching because they reflect the uniqueness of David. One is his obvious enjoyment and pride at using his full name, something he often does in letters and notes to me or Cathy.

It's almost as if he is reveling in how he is an almost-adult, a nearly-adult human being.

> *I keep this particular one on my dresser because it stands for all the other cards and notes and communications that in our family we give each other day in and day out.*

Another is the note's one misspelling, using "your" instead of "you're." David was a victim of a creative-spelling fad that captivated his teachers in his early school years ("Don't worry about the right way, just put down how it sounds. The important thing is to get your ideas on paper."), and there is much about the arrangement of letters in words that he still finds mysterious. As a professional writer, this bugs me to no end. But there's no question that lack of concern with the niceties of grammar and spelling is a part of who David is.

Of course, for me the entire card is touching, with its celebratory use of the Christmas stickers and its many warm, homey scenes of Santa. And what parent wouldn't melt at receiving such a message? Especially one including a sentence as baldly affectionate as "I love you so much." It doesn't get any better than that.

The oddest thing, though, is that this particular card—as touching and as heart-felt as it is—is nothing special. David has given me many other cards just as touching, just as heart-felt. So has Sarah. So, in her own way, has Cathy.

I think I keep this particular one on my dresser because it stands for all the other cards and notes and communications that in our family we give each other day in and day out.

For example, Cathy and the kids recently were away for the weekend on a camping trip. I'm no camper, so I stayed home, reading books and watching TV. But I also took time to use another part of the Print Shop Deluxe software to make a large banner and several small signs that I put up around the house welcoming them home.

For the banner and the signs, I imported photos of each of them. On the signs, I included the message: "I welcome you back to your home with joy at your renewed presence." It was supposed to sound a little stilted to contrast it with the message on the banner. That message, which I borrowed from my newly teenaged daughter, was the image of an eye, the word "lub" and the capital letter U.

It was silly, I admit. Too silly, probably, for anyone not in our family. But it's part of the warp and woof of how we communicate our love for each other all the time.

For Father's Day or my birthday, David and Sarah will make me computer cards and often put up signs and banners. And for Mother's Day. And for Christmas, and for Easter, and for each other's birthdays. Or even, on any ordinary old day, for the pure joy of putting up a sign.

Cathy doesn't go in for all this signage herself. Instead, she pours her love into what she writes in her cards to us or on the ubiquitous "who's-where-when" notes she leaves on the kitchen table for each of us. Her messages overflow with delight and wonder and deep feeling, even when they are of necessity short and to the point.

As with that one sentence in David's card, all of our signs, cards and banners are overtly affectionate. They mirror the way our family relates on a daily basis.

Make no mistake: We often get mad or snippy with one another. And there are times we don't pay attention. At times we hurt one another's feelings or get on one another's nerves. This just means that we're a typical family, as human as the next.

> *In the course of our days we say "I love you" to each other a lot. We're also big on hugs. And kisses.*

But one thing we do amid all the tensions and frictions that living together in a family unavoidably entails is constantly say—both verbally and non-verbally—how much we love each other.

That probably sounds really sappy, and maybe it is. But for us it works. In the course of our days we say "I love you" to each other a lot. We're also big on hugs. And kisses.

Sometimes I wonder when the kids are going to realize that such displays of affection between parents and teenagers aren't considered "cool," but so far they haven't. In fact, as they get older, David and Sarah seem to grow deeper in their enjoyment of showing and receiving love. They relish our cozy time as a family, and they seem to thrive on the mundane words and gestures that manifest our deep feelings for each other. And the same goes for Cathy and me. That's why I keep David's card on my dresser—to remind me of all this.

Even as our two teenagers are drawing away from us to start finding their individual ways in the world, our family knows that there is a tight bond we share. We know it because all four of us constantly express to each other the depth of our love. But what's especially nice for me is the offhand quality of those expressions of affection. They're second nature to each of us. They don't need the accompaniment of violins and trumpets as so often in movies when the words "I love you" are said. In our family, the accompaniment more likely will be the shouldering of a school backpack or the shutting of the refrigerator door. For us, expressions of love are akin to breathing, and what a gift *that* is.

As Sarah and David grow up and move away and start on their own roads of life, Cathy and I won't be able to hug them as much, or kiss them as often, or say, "I love you" (or "eye lub U") to them whenever we want.

But there will be visits. And phone calls. And e-mails and letters. And, yes, there will be hundreds of cards like David's, but none will be more—or less—precious than that one is to me. And, if there's an occasional misspelling or grammatical error, well, so be it.

It's the "lub" that counts. At Christmas...and on any old day.

The Story That Gives Us Stories

Vinita Hampton Wright

I am a storyteller by trade. The word *Christmas* causes me to remember, first of all, that ancient narrative of my faith: God come to earth as a little baby, wrapped up and placed on a straw bed, his young mother miles from her homeland, his father disturbed by dreams. Because the tale is so fantastic, I never get tired of hearing it. Because it is familiar enough that I can imagine myself in the middle of it, I find joy and courage in its retelling.

But when I go a little deeper and think of how Christmas really affects me, other stories emerge as well. They have grown out of that original story, but their characters and settings and plots are from my own life. They are stories of weather and of religion, of tradition, family and food.

This is how true religion works. It plants a grand story into each of our lives and generates new, unique versions of what is beautiful, powerful and eternally true. So we find that the original gift of Christ's arrival carries within it many other gifts, each custom made and wrapped in our individual experiences.

Vinita Hampton Wright   141

For someone who grew up in Kansas, Christmas is the story of winter. The season evokes memories of frosty pastures, of puddles and ditches skimmed with ice. Christmas makes me think also of the sky, because it's the story of a star. When I hear "Star in the east," I see bright glitter upon a cold, black sky. I live in a city now, the lights of which prevent me from seeing many stars. But when I was a child living in a rural community, stars were part of my atmosphere. I would gaze into the night sky at Christmas time and try to imagine that other star, the one that would outshine the North Star, a heavenly body that would stand apart from

From a kid's point of view, the perfect timing was to have a snow-storm once all the relatives had arrived.

Mars and Venus and today's occasional satellite. Church Christmas pageants always happened at night, and I would shiver in my nice dress, stockings and uncomfortable shoes, pausing outside the church to look at the sky. It was not hard, in that imaginative spell that preceded a Christmas play, to see up there, above my little town, a great star that would change our lives.

We had a love-hate relationship with snow at holiday time. We enjoyed it when our town looked like a Currier and Ives print, soft mounds of crystal white rolling between porches and doorways, glowing with the reflection of

Christmas colors. But there was always the hazard of family members having to travel through bad weather to feast and celebrate with us. From a kid's point of view, the perfect timing was to have a snowstorm once all the relatives had arrived. We were all here, and the presents were safe. There was enough food to last for days. So let it snow.

Winter is a hard time of year. It stays darker longer and is often bitter cold. As a child I imagined the Wise Men traveling over snow drifts to see the baby Jesus, the ornamental bells on their long, luxurious robes tinkling in the freezing night. I understand now that Christ's birth was not set against the backdrop of a Kansas December, but I am not that disappointed. I have an adult's understanding of why the Church Fathers would put this celebration smack in the middle of this particular time of year. Winter is a time of death, when the cold and dark are unrelenting and the frail and elderly are most easily overcome. It is often a dangerous time for those who suffer from depression and other trials of the soul.

My husband and I keep the lights in our windows turned on far past Christmas and New Year's. We call them not our Christmas lights but our winter lights, necessary to brighten the long, wearying months until Chicago's spring. But our attitude as pragmatic city dwellers is sparked by visions deep in our memories: blinking lights up and down a farm town's Main Street; a huge, fresh tree in a cozy church parlor, aglow with lights and little angels.

Hardly a Midwesterner of European descent can come to the Christmas season without numerous carols awakening from their summer sleep. Christmas contains not only the story of Christ's birth but the story of how we have remembered it—Advent wreathes, candles in windows, crèches of every size and style, pageants and plays, and the songs that have practically become part of the collective unconscious.

As familiar as we are with the Christmas pageant, as unrecognizable as it can be when children play the lead roles and frayed Sunday school teachers serve as costume and set designers, we enjoy the story just as much, year in and year out. It is at the heart of what we believe about the world. The fact that children embody for half an hour the key persons in the universe makes the Christian religion even more welcoming and palpable. Of course God would appear as a baby (some little girl's doll wrapped in a cast-off baby blanket). Of course a band of unfocused and ornery little boys would be the first people to see angels and find the King of Kings. Of course Mary would let animals in, forgetting their smell and mess. This religion is unbelievable enough that children can understand it, portray it, and practice it. Sometimes it takes a child's version of our sacred stories to remind the adults what the faith is really about.

Christmas is one of the major holy days that define Christianity. Our hymns of the season reach into souls who don't even care about faith. Our amateur reenactments represent well how the God of the universe has entrusted so much, so lovingly, to human beings. Christmas is about, most of all, God coming down to visit. Back where I come from, visiting is still built into one's lifestyle. When folks stop by, you give them the comfortable chair and find something for them to eat. You may dash back to the bedroom to put on a nicer shirt. You put on your best manners as well. The great Christmas visit is about people at their best, capable in their hearts of recognizing when the divine has stepped inside the door.

Christmas is the great excuse to create rituals. Christmas rituals give birth to even more rituals. My family provides an excellent example of this.

My father loved to cook. And every year he made fruitcakes for every family in our extended family. No, these were not the fruitcakes that comedians joke about being passed along year after year. These were made by hand with the best ingredients and aged in liquor-soaked cheesecloth for weeks. Dad's fruitcakes were much anticipated on both sides of the family.

My father worked a factory job. There was no discretionary income in our family. So he would begin buying the currants and candied fruit in the summer, stocking up a little at a time. It was impossible to do this regarding pecans, because they must be fresh and pecans are harvested in autumn. Fortunately, my mother's aunt and uncle had a farm about fifteen miles from town, and out in its timberland were well-aged pecan groves. So when the air became chilly and the leaves were turning, we would go pecan picking. Mom, Aunt Veta, Grandma, Dad and we kids, armed with large coffee cans, would scavenge the ground in the shade of those tall trees and pick up pounds and pounds of freshly fallen pecans. At the end of the day, Uncle Clarence would build a bonfire in the pasture and Aunt Veta would bring out the wieners and marshmallows.

No one bakes those fruitcakes anymore, but I have taken it upon myself to recreate the Christmas breads.

Through the rest of autumn, my father would sit in his chair in front of the television with nutcracker and picks. First he would crack all the pecans and put them in large plastic bags, which he would line up beside his chair. Then the painstaking work of picking out nutmeats would begin. Through Sunday football and evening news and movies of the week, the bags of cracked nuts would become canisters of golden pecan halves ready for the holiday baking. About a month before Christmas, he would make the fruitcakes, and they would age until the holiday.

My father loved Christmas almost more than is humanly natural. But during most of my childhood he was rarely home on Christmas Day. He worked at a bakery that produced sliced bread, dinner rolls, and buns for hot dogs and hamburgers. Because it was a major food producer, they always needed higher volume at holiday time. Dad worked the night shift for many years, and he would arrive home in the middle of Christmas Day.

He compensated for his absence on Christmas morning by leaving on the kitchen counter a special breakfast bread he had made that Mom could toast under the broiler for her and us girls. Some years it was Stollen, others it was cinnamon bread or pull-apart pecan rolls. But always there was something, perfectly shaped and drizzled with powdered sugar frosting. My sister and I awoke at earliest light and tore into our presents, and then Mom toasted the bread and served it with cocoa.

Every family that celebrates Christmas has its own traditions. We had numerous other practices—buying and decorating a tree, playing Christmas LPs nonstop, and making many tins of cookies and candies. But now I am older than my father was back then, and he has been in heaven for eleven years. No one bakes those fruitcakes anymore, but I have taken it upon myself to recreate the Christmas breads. These traditions are the ones I remember first.

My family's saga is told in a succession of Christmas photographs. Most of us didn't bother to pull out cameras except for events such as births, graduations and the occasional new car. But at Christmas we did our best to fill in the gaps.

There's a particularly poignant photograph tucked away

in my mother's house: five generations seated together on Grandma's orange sofa—Great-Aunt Dee, Grandma, Mom, my sister Valinda, and her son Korey. I regretted that I never submitted that one to the local paper.

By looking through our snapshot history, I see more clearly now what marked our family at holiday time. For instance, we enjoyed the holiday more when there were new babies. Each baby's first Christmas was a very big deal. One year, there were four new babies at Grandma's house, causing near euphoria. All were dressed up in tiny plush outfits, warm wiggly bundles of velvet reds and greens. We posed them all together for pictures, each child held in a standing position by arms that belonged to some adult whose face remained off camera. These children would also enter school at the same time; a few years ago I went to their multiple high school graduations. Now they've begun having their own babies.

Our joy was muted, however, any year we had lost a loved one. The photos from that particular Christmas became the first record of the family without Great-Grandma, Uncle Bud, Dad...whomever.

I scan these faded tableaux and see younger, smoother faces—people before retirement years, before the stress of worrying over children expanded to the stress of worrying over grandchildren. I see in other faces the strain of a divorce endured, the marks of long illness, or the evidence of a drinking habit gone worse. I see pairs of people who aren't pairs anymore, and I see gatherings of children who have grown up and gone away. I see a long departed grand-parent, nearly obliterated by a foreground full of kids and wrapping paper, who would ask to see each and every gift that every person received and who waited patiently for her own yearly supply of body lotion and talcum powder.

Now that my two sisters and I live in three separate places—one in the hometown, one in Los Angeles and one in Chicago—the Christmas photos reveal who was able to make the trek back to Kansas any particular year. We can look back now and know which year it was according to who is absent in the photos. There are now multiple sets of photos, of multiple celebrations in their respective locations, mailed back and forth so that no one has to miss out completely on watching the little ones open their gifts. Not only are there multiple photo shoots within my family of origin but also various Christmas locations within my family of husband, two stepsons and a granddaughter. We all gather as best we can as many times as we can, to spend a day at least with the Atlanta kids, the Portland kids, the Kansas grandparents, or the Oklahoma or Florida siblings.

So we have many photographers now. Sometimes our photos are sent by way of e-mail. But they serve the same purpose. We normally don't think to size up our families and line up relatives in the way we are compelled to do at Christmas time, so this holiday is—along with many other things—a gathering time, a summing up, a photo essay designed to bring a whole year back to vivid memory.

Allow me to be frivolous now and dwell upon food. This is appropriate when you consider that the Christian faith has at its center a holy feast. Jesus understood that everybody has to eat and has to do it every day. Our stomachs remind us every few hours that we are anything but self-sustaining. The Holy Eucharist reminds us that our souls as well as our bodies need regular care and feeding.

Grandma was at her zenith when putting on a holiday spread.

I doubt that Grandma ever thought about the Eucharist while peeling potatoes before dawn as she prepared the Christmas dinner. For one thing, Grandma was an Assemblies of God Christian who probably never used the word "Eucharist." But her staying power was fueled by ancient longings and everlasting dreams. She, after all, had barely survived the Great Depression. She was matriarch of a clan that included the families of five siblings, all within a day's drive. At one time, her mother had earned a living as chief cook for a wealthy couple on Chicago's north lakeshore. Food was what kept people going. It gathered them in one place and, once gathered, they visited and caught up with one another's lives. Eating a good meal made folks feel safe and happy.

Grandma was at her zenith when putting on a holiday spread. She would chop and fry and bake and arrange, alone in her kitchen, while mentally drawing up the plan for who would sit at which table (kitchen or dining room?) or card table (dining room or living room?) and which dishes would be located where. She waited impatiently for anyone who arrived even a few minutes late, eliciting phone calls to this house and that to hurry families along. Once seated, a person had no choice but to tunnel out with spoon and fork through three kinds of meat; vegetable casseroles (vegetables were made edible by cream soups, cheeses and sauces in the way fruits were presented only in the context of ice cream, pastry or jello); three kinds of potatoes; relishes; rolls; dressing; and a whole pot of real gravy, full of giblets and plenty salty.

She watched us like a foreman overseeing construction of the Panama Canal, with eyes that required glasses for reading yet somehow latched onto the single hand that passed down the chicken-noodle-cheese casserole without ladling some onto the plate. If a dish got held up in heavy traffic at one end of the table, she was there to rescue it back into service, all the while giving a steady rhythm of orders, directing individuals to the dishes they had somehow missed or hadn't taken enough from.

Two hours after dinner, Grandma became the Dessert Commando. Wherever you were, reclined and belching helplessly like a foundered horse, she would hunt you down and demand that you choose your sweet. Desserts were identified by their creators. There was Virginia's pumpkin pie, Veta's pecan pie, Blanche's pineapple cake, and Grandma's own apple pie, chocolate cake and coconut-cream-cheese-walnut supreme. There was also Cindy's caramel corn, Lorraine's fudge and Debra's homemade cherry chocolates (also a ton or so of cookies in many styles), but these things did not count as dessert; they were merely snacks.

There was no small portion in Grandma's mentality. She could take four pies and divide them among forty people so that each person got a fourth of a pie. Jesus could have taken lessons from her.

Which is why I'm sure that Jesus understands the holiday feast of Christmas. He understands the comfort of abundance and the nurturing properties of food. His coming to earth created Christmas, but the holy infant grew up and walked among us, enjoying the pungent flavor of roasted fish over a beach fire, the rich offerings of wedding feasts, the breads and sweets and savory meats served up by the hands of Jewish mothers and aunts and grandmothers during celebrations of family and faith.

God understands our relief when the harvest has been brought in, safe and sound, to sustain us through the winter. God does notice our overwhelming sense of thankfulness as we gather around the communal table and see those who have survived the storms and change of one more year. And I don't think that the Good Lord minds when we overeat at holiday time. Christmas is, as much as anything, the story of extravagance. We celebrate—through songs and colored lights and fancy breads—in order to hope. We tell our favorite stories, mugs of cocoa in hand, in order to remember.

Afterword

id you ever wonder what leaping lords, French hens, swimming swans and especially a partridge that apparently refuses to leave its pear tree have to do with Christmas?

No, "The Twelve Days of Christmas" wasn't an early Nieman-Marcus catalogue. The carol actually comes from a time when Roman Catholics in England were not permitted to practice their faith openly.

According to my pastor emeritus, Father Leo Mahon, the carol "has two levels of meaning: the surface meaning plus a hidden meaning known only to members of the church at the time. Each element in the carol had a code word for a religious reality that the children in the church were supposed to remember."

Here, according to Fr. Mahon, is what each of the twelve "gifts" of Christmas stood for:

- The partridge in a pear tree was Jesus Christ.
- Two turtle doves were the Old and New Testaments.
- Three French hens were faith, hope and love.
- Four calling birds were the four gospels of Matthew, Mark, Luke and John.
- Five golden rings were the Torah, the first five books of the Old Testament.
- Six geese a-laying were the six days of creation.
- Seven swans a-swimming were the gifts of the Holy Spirit: prophesy, serving, teaching, exhortation, contribu-

tion, leadership and mercy.

- Eight maids a-milking were the eight beatitudes.
- Nine ladies dancing were the fruits of the Holy Spirit: love, joy, peace, patience, kindness, goodness, faithfulness, gentleness and self-control.
- Ten lords a-leaping were the ten commandments.
- Eleven pipers piping were the eleven faithful apostles.
- Twelve drummers drumming were the twelve points of belief in the Apostle's Creed.

What strikes me about this obscure bit of church history is that the gifts of Christmas have *always* stood for much deeper realities—from the gifts of gold, frankincense and myrrh brought by the three wise men to the playing of the drum by the little drummer boy to the hair combs and watch fob given to each other by the married couple in the O. Henry story.

Christmas is about giving gifts, to be sure. The news that the infinite God actually became a human being is too good for any Christian to contain. We feel compelled to spread it to everyone we know (and even to people we do not know) in the form of gifts each December. But these gifts are always more than what they seem on the surface. Like the gifts whose stories appear in this book, they assure us that a loving God is with us at all times and that we can experience that God through the material "stuff" of our daily world.

And it is this belief in the divine presence that makes *every* Christmas merry, no matter what else might be going on in our lives.

About the Contributors

Father James Stephen (Jeffrey) Behrens is a priest of the Archdiocese of Newark, New Jersey, and the author of *Grace Is Everywhere* and *Memories of Grace.*

Alice Camille is a religious educator and lecturer and the author of *Invitation to Catholicism* and *Seven Last Words: Reflections for Today's Believers.*

Delle Chatman is the Director of the Media Arts Division of the National High School Institute at Northwestern University and the author of *The Death of a Parent* and *The Unteachable Ten.*

Carol DeChant is the author of *Momma's Enchanted Supper: Stories for the Long Evenings of Advent.*

Kass Dotterweich is the managing editor for Sheed and Ward and the author of many books, including *25 Stories for Sharing Faith with Teens.*

Fredric Hang is a senior trainer for the Great Books Foundation and the screenwriter of the video program *Stories of the Human Spirit.*

Father Patrick Hannon, CSC, is the principal and a teacher of literature at Notre Dame High School for Boys in Morton Grove, Illinois and the author of a forthcoming book of stories about prayer.

Michael Leach is the publisher of Orbis Books and the co-author of *I Like Being Catholic* and *I Like Being Married.*

Tom McGrath is the editorial director and publisher of TrueQuest Communications and the author of *Raising Faith-*

Gregory F. Augustine Pierce

Filled Kids and *Daily Meditations (with Scripture) for Busy Parents.*

Patrick T. Reardon is a reporter for the *Chicago Tribune* and the author of *Daily Meditations (with Scripture) for Busy Dads* and *Starting Out: Reflections for Young People.*

John Shea is a theologian and storyteller and the author of *Stories of God* and *Elijah at the Wedding Feast and Other Tales: Stories of the Human Spirit.*

Vinita Hampton Wright is acquisitions editor for Loyola Press and the author of two novels, *Grace at Bender Springs* and *Velma Still Cooks in Leeway.*

Acknowledgments

Y ou cannot compile a collection of great, original stories unless you know a lot of great, original storytellers. Fortunately, I do.

Thanks to James (Jeff) Behrens, Alice Camille, Delle Chatman, Carol DeChant, Kass Dotterweich, Fred Hang, Pat Hannon, Mike Leach, Tom McGrath, Pat Reardon, John Shea and Vinita Wright—first for being such good friends and colleagues and secondly for sharing their stories with me and with you.

I also want to thank Luke and Matthew and the billions of Christians over the centuries since the birth of Jesus who have kept alive "The Story That Gives Us Stories," as Vinita Wright calls it. They have reminded us of this central truth of Christmas: No matter what material form it takes, love is always more than it seems.

And finally to you, dear reader, I offer my sincere appreciation. For a book is truly complete only when someone has read it from the beginning to the end.

Contributor books from ACTA Publications

James Stephen Behrens
- *Grace Is Everywhere: Reflections of an Aspiring Monk* (160 page paperback, $12.95)
- *Memories of Grace: Portraits from the Monastery* (160 page paperback, $12.95)

Alice Camille
- *Invitation to Catholicism: Beliefs + Teachings + Practices* (240 page paperback, $9.95)
- *Seven Last Words: Lenten Reflections for Today's Believers* (96 page paperback, $6.95)

Delle Chatman
- *The Death of a Parent: Reflections for Adults Mourning the Loss of a Father or Mother* (128 page paperback, $9.95)

Kass Dotterweich
- *25 Stories for Sharing Faith with Teens* (96 page workbook, $19.95)

Tom McGrath
- *Daily Meditations (with Scripture) for Busy Parents* (240 page paperback, $9.95)

Patrick T. Reardon
- *Daily Meditations (with Scripture) for Busy Dads* (368 page paperback, $9.95)
- *Starting Out: Reflections for Young People* (112 page paperback, $5.95)

John Shea
- *Elijah at the Wedding Feast and Other Tales* (160 page paperback, $12.95)

Available from booksellers or call 800-397-2282